Glen & Nick have written a masterpiece that demystifies the world of investing, offering clear guidance and actionable steps for readers of any level. If you're new to money and investing or if you're after some more advanced strategies and ideas, this book will be invaluable.

—**Victoria Devine, author of bestselling book** *She's on the Money*

Very few books do what Glen and Nick have been able to achieve: creating genuine impact that will last you a lifetime. You won't want to put this down and you'll be thanking your past self every single day for the learnings you took away. A must read for everyone.

—**Simran Kaur, international bestselling author and creator of Girls That Invest**

Investing can be daunting, but Glen and Nick's book breaks it down into clear, manageable steps that anyone can follow. From understanding your motivations to mastering advanced strategies, each chapter offers valuable insights and practical advice. Whether you're just starting out or looking to refine your approach, this book is an essential guide. Their expertise shines through, making complex concepts accessible and actionable. Highly recommended for anyone who is serious about building a solid investment portfolio.

—**Bryce and Alec,** *Equity Mates Investing Podcast*

Learning how to make your money work for you gives you freedom and more options in life. Investing can sometimes feel scary and complicated, but Glen and Nick are experts at demystifying it all to leave you more confident and knowledgeable.

—**Tim Duggan, bestselling author of** *Work Backwards* **and** *Cult Status*

T0205112

Glen and Nick bring the same breezy style to investing they display on the podcast. *The Quick Start Guide to Investing* is an accessible, fluff-free guide to everything you need to know and everything you need to do to get started investing successfully. This book delivers all the great investment feels you want without the Reddit Software Bro attitude you don't. An essential handbook for new investors — don't enter the market without it.

—Vince Scully, financial adviser and author of *Live The Life You Want With The Money You Have*

Glen and Nick have made smart investing simple and within reach for so many people. *The Quick Start Guide to Investing* will get you out of your own way and finally taking action on your plans to take investing seriously.

—Emma Edwards, author of *Good With Money* and founder of The Broke Generation

I'm way too rich and don't have time to read this book but I'm sure it's fabulous.

—Alright Hey, Australia's Biggest Glamazon

Investing can seem intimidating. But Glen and Nick do a killer job demystifying this crucial topic. They'll help you create a simple but effective plan for your financial future. If you want to grow wealth but are unsure how to proceed, this book will deliver much-needed clarity.

—Joel & Matt, *How To Money* podcast

Glen and Nick transform complex concepts into a easy-to-digest guide that will set up your financial future.

—Alisha Aitken-Radburn, media personality and author of *The Villain Edit*

Glen & Nick turn the complex world of investing into a refreshingly simple and practical journey in this outstanding book. An indispensable guide for anyone looking to make smarter, more confident investment decisions!

—**James Millard, financial adviser and author of**
Insufficient Funds

My eyes and ears used to glaze over when the nightly news turned to 'Finance', it was foreign acronyms and buzzwords for 'rich people'. I wanted to try investing in shares but it was overwhelming and I had no idea where to start. *The Quick-Start Guide to Investing* breaks it down into bite-size chunks in accessible language. This introduction into investing built my confidence and saw me put my first $5K into a Vanguard Investor Account - my real-life penny drop moment. Empowerment through knowledge!

—**Laura P, laywer and podcast listener**

Even if you've already done a bit of investing, this book is for you if you want to start taking it seriously. All in one you'll get the fundamentals in place, make great decisions and then take it to the next level with advanced strategies. I'll be buying copies for my whole family!

—**Sarah Smith, HR manager and podcast listener**

the quick start guide to investing

LEARN HOW TO INVEST
simpler, smarter & sooner

GLEN JAMES & NICK BRADLEY

WILEY

First published in 2024 by John Wiley & Sons Australia, Ltd
Level 4, 600 Bourke St, Melbourne, Victoria 3000, Australia

Typeset in Tisa Pro 10/16pt

ISBN: 978-1-394-19463-6

A catalogue record for this book is available from the National Library of Australia

Cover design by Jason Knight (www.askjasonknight.com)
Figure 2.6: Illustration © Visual Generation / Adobe Stock

Disclaimer
The material in this publication is of the nature of general comment only, and does not represent professional advice. It is not intended to provide specific guidance for particular circumstances and it should not be relied on as the basis for any decision to take action or not take action on any matter which it covers. Readers should obtain professional advice where appropriate, before making any such decision. To the maximum extent permitted by law, the authors and publisher disclaim all responsibility and liability to any person, arising directly or indirectly from any person taking or not taking action based on the information in this publication.

Any advice is general financial advice only which does not take into account your objectives, financial situation or needs. Because of that, you should consider if the advice is appropriate to you and your needs, before acting on the information. If you do choose to buy a financial product read the product disclosure statement (PDS) and target market determination (TMD) and obtain appropriate financial advice tailored to your needs. SYMO interactive Pty Ltd trading as this is money & Glen James are authorised representatives of MoneySherpa Pty Ltd which holds financial services licence 451289.

We acknowledge the Traditional Custodians of the land on which we reside, and pay respects to their Elders past, present and emerging.

We extend that respect to Aboriginal and Torres Strait Islander peoples who may read this book.

Contents

Hi, we're so glad you're here!

This book is an investment. An investment into knowledge, but more importantly, an investment into you and your future. We'd like to start by setting the scene: letting you know what we're about, where we have come from and what you can expect. As this book has been written by two authors, we have decided, for the majority of the book, to each write different parts rather than having just one 'voice'. We'll tell you who wrote what before you read each section or chapter.

A note from Glen

Investing is easy. I'll show you how. You could download an investment app (popular ones are Superhero and Sharesies), open an account, transfer some money over to your account, buy the ETF IOZ and *voilà!* You now own 200 of the top Australian companies with only one transaction. You have some diversification so your risk is spread, and your record keeping and tax reporting is taken care of each year. You might want to do this with as much money as you can, as regularly as you can, for as long as you can. And you might try not to sell—consider reinvesting the dividends/distributions instead. Over time you'll build so much wealth you won't know what to do with it all!

That's one of the easiest ways to buy a diversified portfolio of Australian shares. But there's more you need to understand about building a diversified portfolio ... and more about why you're even investing. You see, when it comes to all things money and investing it can be a trap to fall into solution mode right away. That's why we'll start with your 'why'—your reason for investing—in chapter 1.

I'll aim not only to get you invested fast, but also to help you understand everything you need to know when it comes to the basics of investing. Then my co-author, Nick, will take over and provide you with some more advanced strategies that might scratch an itch you have to get more involved in other investing strategies.

I've been an investor for around 20 years. For 13 of those I was a licensed financial adviser working with clients face-to-face and I have come to learn that the easiest part of investing is the investing itself. The hardest part is continuing to be invested and removing yourself from the week-on-week, month-on-month processes, fads and distractions. That is, setting yourself up financially so that once money is committed to your investing account, it stays invested and isn't withdrawn to pay for car insurance, holidays or other things.

I want you to be wealthy. I want you to be secure. But I want you to do it the right way. Like everything in life, there isn't actually 'the way'—there's 'a way' to arrive at a location or solution. We see this book as 'a way'. Nick and I have a similar investing philosophy and we're both about building wealth for the long term. However, we do things differently along the way.

In my first book, *Sort your money out & get invested*, I shared the story of my first investment in shares, which was an absolute trainwreck.

It resulted in a loss of 40 per cent of the capital I had invested after breaking every rule in the book! So, since the days of the 18-year-old Glen, my strategy has somewhat changed (I'll tell you all about that in the coming chapters). My new strategy allows me to focus on the income-generation side of wealth building and having a somewhat set-and-forget portfolio set-up.

You'll find with all the online noise in groups and on Reddit, that the chatter often lands in the area of brokerage fees, investment platforms and whether or not to invest in, say, IOZ or A200 (which basically cost the same and both track the top 200 companies listed on the Australian share market). In my own experience, getting into the weeds with such issues is like not being able to proceed with a dinner order at a restaurant because you can't decide whether to order tap water or bottled water—it's like majoring in the minor, if you know what I mean.

So why have we written this book? Well, I host a podcast—*this is money*—that has a large community of listeners, and ever since I started it in 2018 the number-one thing people wanted to know about is investing in shares. Since this topic was popular, I asked Nick to host a dedicated podcast. I'll be the first to say I'm not an academic—nor do I want to be. And I can't speak for my co-author—though I will!—but he isn't an academic either. So think of this as a street-smart guide to investing. We really wanted to write a book that's full of useful information, along with some prompts to challenge your thinking or to make you more focused.

Nick, who hosts our investing podcast—*this is investing*—is originally from Alaska and now resides in Columbus, Ohio in the United States. You might think that it's weird to have someone in the United States co-author an investing book for a predominantly Australian audience. However, it attests to the fact that the language of investing is truly international. Nick is a very close friend of mine whom

I've known for many years and I trust him explicitly to speak to my podcast community. He has a lot of experience and curiosity when it comes to investing.

The cool thing is that while there are different accents to each language, it's all the same when it comes to investing. One product in Australia may give you access to an international index (language) and you can get the same product in, say, the United States with a different name (accent) and with the same exposure. This is akin to my current hire car while writing this part of the book in 'the States'. It's a Chevrolet Cruze — the Australian version is the Holden Cruze. The world is truly becoming globalised when it comes to physical products. However, it kind of always has been when it comes to investing. An ETF with the ticker code IVV can be purchased on the ASX (domiciled to Australia), giving you weighted exposure to the S&P 500 index, which is the top 500 listed companies across all exchanges in the United States. This ETF is provided by the international investment powerhouse BlackRock and its iShares S&P 500 fund can also be purchased on the NYSE with the same ticker code: IVV: the same product, available in both the United States and Australia. (If some of the investing terms I'm using are making your head spin, you'll find definitions for the trickier ones at the end of this introduction.)

Another reason why I wanted Nick to be involved with this book is that we need to pay attention to the United States when it comes to investing. I'm reluctant to say this to my friend, but he can be, and is, useful to have around. Nick is on the ground in the United States. While we can get information about investing online, Nick is immersed in it day-to-day and has a genuine passion for investing.

To give you some more perspective, you've likely used a product today made by Apple or Microsoft, or scrolled Instagram or Facebook.

You may watch Netflix or Disney+ tonight or google how to cook up some fava beans or where to buy a nice bottle of Chianti (extremely niche joke, for those who know!). These companies are listed in the United States and have true global reach.

To drive this home further, the total gross domestic product (GDP) of Australia is approximately $1.5 trillion US, whereas the state of California alone has a GDP of $3.5 trillion US! This is why I've always been inclined to 'get off the island' when it comes to investing and learning more—there really is a bigger world out there when it comes to money and investing than an island in the South Pacific.

Now, the truly unique thing about Australia is that though we're small, we pack a punch. We're part of the top 20 economies in the world. While this may be off the back of digging up most of the island and selling it overseas (namely iron ore and coal to China), there are many quality public companies listed on the ASX that have provided long-term stable returns.

Australia is a great place to start one's investing journey because it's relatively simple to get started here. You understand the brands and companies because you've grown up shopping at Woolworths, perhaps banking at the Commonwealth Bank, or you've had a Telstra mobile plan forever. This sense of familiarity can help you when starting out.

Whenever I speak or when writing my previous books, I've encouraged people to look for one thing to take away and implement. Generally, if you have a 'penny-drop moment' and change just one behaviour or start something new in your life—or even stop doing something that is negatively impacting you or not taking you towards your financial or lifestyle goals—that's a win. Don't get overwhelmed: look for the one thing you can start or stop and the rest is a wonderful bonus.

On a final note, Nick and I have an interesting dry and sarcastic sense of humour, which you'll pick up on as you read this book. We're very good friends with a robust friendship, so we have fun talking about serious topics in a way that may be different from the norm, including having a jab at each other along the way.

I'll hand you over to Nick now to bore you with a bit of his story and what his vibe is for this book. Then we'll explain a few of the investing terms you've already come across in this introduction, after which we'll get right into it! If you learn anything from this book, I'll take the credit. If there are mistakes or things you disagree with, blame Nick. 😊

Glen.

A note from Nick

How I got interested in investing is a simple story. In 1998 I was in grade 8, living in Anchorage, Alaska. Every year the local newspaper, *Anchorage Daily News*, had a stock-picking competition for all eighth-grade students in the area who were enrolled in an economics course.

The premise of the competition was that you had $50 000 to invest in stocks, and whoever chose the best stocks with the best performance by the end of the semester won the competition. Being eighth-grade boys, many of my friends selected stocks such as Coca-Cola, Playboy and various companies like those. I remember choosing Coca-Cola, but I thought I would get in trouble from my mother if I followed suit and invested in Playboy like my friends, so I invested in a couple of companies that ended with 'soft'. I didn't do any research, I just picked them. In fact, it didn't dawn on me until later in the semester that 'soft' stood for 'software'. One of the 'soft' companies I selected was Microsoft, and if my memory serves me correctly the other company was called TibcoSoft.

By the end of the semester, Coca-Cola was probably up 1 to 2 per cent, Microsoft was up 20 to 30 per cent and the little-known company called TibcoSoft was up nearly 100 per cent, with a stock split as well, so I owned more shares than I'd started with. I ended up winning the stock-picking challenge, and my love of the stock market and all things investing was officially embedded into my young psyche. (For those of you for whom the term 'stock split' is new, this occurs when the number of a company's outstanding shares are divided or 'split', which in turn reduces the price per share without changing the overall market capitalisation of the company.)

As an eighth grader who fancied himself as a stock-picking savant, I told my dad he should invest in these software companies. I checked the newspaper every single day to see the performance of the stock market. I remember being upset at weekends because my investments in my fake stock-picking game were not updated in the paper on weekends. But I was never able to convince my dad to invest in these newly founded internet companies, a decision that was both good and bad. An investment in Microsoft in 1998 would have ended up being very lucrative had it been held until 2024. But an investment in TibcoSoft would have ended up a total loss as they went bankrupt in the dot-com bust just two years later.

Since I was only in eighth grade and had no money of my own to invest, I went back to my normal activities of hockey and chasing girls. But the seed for the stock market was planted in my heart.

Growing up in Alaska, many people work in the oil fields located in the Arctic Circle. I dabbled in the dark arts of petroleum drilling in the winter after high school, but realised this wasn't the life for me. So I enrolled in a business management university course that included finance classes.

Post-college I started working for a securities bank, got my investment advisers licence and, just like that, my love for investing returned ... but the year was 2006 and little did I know how hard life was going to get just 15 short months later.

The Global Financial Crisis (GFC)

My fun run as an upstart investment adviser was met very quickly with a grave lesson from the stock market. A 'black swan' event was on the horizon and, looking back, it seemed obvious that reckless spending on multiple mortgages on multiple houses at a time was going to be a big deal. At the time, no-one except a few shrewd hedge funds was paying attention. (See *The Big Short*, a movie on the GFC for more info.)

In December 2007, everything started happening at once. The stock market was in free fall. In fact, it halted trading for a bit to slow down the panic. The use of 'circuit breakers' to halt trading is very rare—they were implemented in 1987 as a result of the 1987 NYSE crash. These breakers had only been used in 1997 and again on 11 September 2001. So, to say they are rare is an understatement. Seeing huge historical Wall Street institutions such as Bear Stearns and Lehman Brothers, followed by others, go out of business was rattling to the economy and the average retail investor.

I was receiving calls practically non-stop from worried and scared clients who didn't know what to do. It is in times like these that your resolve is tested, and your plan is tested even more. I tell you this story to say that I was scared. I was an investment adviser and I was scared. Seeing your retirement account fall by 30 to 40 per cent is not a fun feeling.

But we all survived. People who had a good plan and kept investing not only made their money back, they bought one of the great stock-market sales of all time. The investments they made while the market was falling became some of the best money they have ever invested. Warren Buffet, the 'Oracle of Omaha' (Omaha is a small city in Nebraska), invested $5 billion US to 'save' Goldman Sachs and to show the American people and the world that investing during the GFC was not only 'safe' but wise. At the time it seemed like one of the richest men in the world was saving Wall Street. But he wasn't investing because he's an altruist. He looked at Goldman Sachs, saw their leadership, their plan and their potential future and he invested. Just a few years later that $5 billion was worth $8 billion. Investing in good companies, broad indexes and solid markets will never go out of style.

That's why we're writing this book: to give you some ideas on how to make and stick to a good plan. Seek out solid companies that you like and ascertain whether they are good investments or a flash in the pan. And then work out how can you dig in, get your hands dirty and start building wealth through the stock market.

Before we begin

This book is not a textbook, and I do not claim that it is. It is not to be used as a substitute for formal education or analysis of share investing, market analysis, accounting or taxation. We have on purpose kept away  from a deep level of technical, financial information and detail. It may also be one of the first investing books that does not detail 'franking credits' for Australian shares and their tax treatment.

We wrote this book for the person who has an interest in investing in shares and ETFs to build wealth and those who want a quick start and need a framework to follow.

We want to teach you about learning to invest — much like learning to drive when you were 16 years old. This is the car; these are the 'go' and the 'stop' pedals; watch out for stop signs; don't speed; and stay on the look out. You've got the basics of how to drive and are now a successful, licensed driver without having to learn the mechanics of how an internal combustion engine operates. If you're a mechanical purist, it will likely annoy you that people aren't taught about mechanics when they learn to drive. Rest assured, not everyone is like you (hehe) and there are ways people can learn more, should they be interested in doing so.

We do, however, want to highlight some of the baseline investing terminology and acronyms that you need to know if you're new to investing. This will help you hit the ground running and make sense of this introduction to our book. Here we go!

Security

A security is a financial instrument that has a monetary value and can be traded. Such as shares, bonds and ETFs.

Stock exchanges

Let's touch on three main stock exchanges for now:

- ASX: Australian Securities Exchange. This is where the majority of Australian public companies list their shares to allow those shares to be bought/sold and this is done so via a broker that connects to the exchange.

- NYSE: New York Stock Exchange. The oldest and biggest stock exchange in the United States.

- *NASDAQ:* National Association of Securities Dealers Automated Quotations. This stock market is a newer exchange in the United States. It is second in size to the NYSE; however, it was the first to be completely electronic and many tech companies chose to list on this exchange.

Index/weighted index and rebalancing

An index is effectively a list of companies. This could be as simple as the top 500 companies by size or the top 20 semiconductor companies or *insert niche here*. Most indexes are weighted.

Let's use an example of an investment into a 'market capitalised weighted index' fund. Say you wish to invest $10 000 into a fictitious fund that tracks the three biggest sporting goods retailers in the United States.

This index is called the 'Big 3 Sport Index', or simply the 'B3S index' and was created by the fictitious fund manager Driftwood Capital Partners to get a sense of the activity of sporting supply sales as high school sports, college sports and recreational sporting equipment sales are a good pulse check of the discretionary spending of middle America. You have decided you want exposure to these big three retailers but you are happy to just set-and-forget with a one-stop shop and let your investment do whatever the index does.

Driftwood Capital Partners created an ETF that also tracks its index and has a ticker code of 'B3S'. The investment into the 'B3S' ETF would be as follows:

'B3S' index:

- Retailer A is worth $2 billion (57% of index)

- Retailer B is worth $1 billion (29% of index)

- Retailer C is worth $500 million (14% of index)

Total market capitalisation of the 'B3S' index is $3.5 billion (100%).

Effective exposure of your $10 000 invested:

- Retailer A: $5700 (or 57%)

- Retailer B: $2900 (or 29%)

- Retailer C: $1400 (or 14%)

Each quarter Driftwood Capital Partners would review the weightings of the index and, if needed, change the allocation to each retailer. This is called rebalancing. There could be a retailer that grows to become worth more than Retailer C and that would mean Retailer C would leave the index and be replaced. Another thing that may happen at a quarterly rebalance is that Retailer B could take market share from Retailer A and represent 33 per cent of the index — up from 29 per cent — meaning Retailer A's exposure would be reduced to 53 per cent of the index.

Driftwood Capital Partners charges a fee of 0.60 per cent, or $60 per year, for managing the $10 000 worth of funds invested.

Most indexes that we discuss in this book and that are out there in the wild are weighted, unless otherwise specified.

S&P 500

Standard & Poor's (S&P) 500 is a weighted index of the top 500 companies in the United States. On all exchanges, Standard & Poor's is an American stock research company. It effectively created and owns the index.

Dow Jones (or Dow)

The Dow Jones Industrial Average is a weighted index of the top 30 companies in the United States (on all exchanges). This is one of the oldest indexes and is sometimes seen as a good guide for what the total market is doing. However, many say the S&P 500 is a better representation.

Exchange Traded Fund (ETF)

This is an investment structure that can be purchased and traded (bought/sold) on a stock exchange. Within the structure, the fund manager will either manage investments (actively) or provide you with exposure to an index. In almost all instances, what is on the label is in the can.

Stocks / shares / equities

These all mean the same thing and they are commonly inter-changed depending on the vibe of the writing or conversation! Generally, Americans stay 'stock' and Aussies say 'shares', but most people use all three.

Private equity

This is a style of investment management. Generally, an unlisted entity that collects money from investors and then purchases different companies and startup ventures. They would buy unlisted companies or get a good price for a listed company and make it private (remove it from public exchange). They may 'renovate' a company and sell it again for a profit. Usually, high risk/high reward territory.

Hedge

A hedge is like insurance for your investments. It should be non-correlated so if your investment goes down it would possibly keep going up to offset any mid-term losses on your other investments.

Hedge fund

A hedge fund is where a money manager can take on high-net-worth, qualified clients — typically over $10 million in net worth. They use the word 'hedge' because the money managers are not beholden to a long, only-investment strategy. They are able to use various investments to make money in bearish or bullish stock markets.

Domicile / domiciled

This is an important word that we want you to be familiar with. Think of it as 'home'. When you purchase shares and ETFs, they have a domicile. This is the country they are registered in for taxation. It is important to understand this because technology now allows us to buy shares and ETFs in any country. Like my (Glen's) previous example, the IVV ETF can be purchased in Australia (ASX) and the United States (NYSE). If you buy ETFs or shares not domiciled in Australia, you will need to complete international tax and ownership forms. This can be burdensome. If you wanted to buy direct shares in, say, Apple, you have no choice but to buy this domiciled to the United States and complete their tax form (W-8BEN) as there is only one Apple.

Broker

You may have seen *The Wolf of Wall Street*, which documents the exploits of a stockbroker in the 1980s physically calling people, selling them shares and acting as a middle man while taking a clip on each transaction. Nowadays, this is all done electronically and you will need a broker or platform to access markets where you can buy your shares. Brokers and platforms allow you to have different entities own the account—such as your own name, joint names and some even allow you to operate their service via your superannuation or retirement savings. Brokers have cash accounts that you can deposit money into. They then place trades during the opening hours of the relevant exchange on your behalf. Brokerage accounts in Australia do not track your investing, dividend/distribution reinvesting and buys/sells for tax purposes. So you need to be 100 per cent on top of your paperwork both year-on-year for annual tax returns and over the life of the ownership for asset sales.

Platform

A platform is a one-stop shop. I (Glen) love and use platforms myself. Platforms also have a bank account that you can transfer money into. However, the assets that you purchase are held in trust on your behalf (much like your superannuation) and each year the platform provides you with a consolidated tax report so you don't have to worry about the record keeping yourself. Hallelujah! The platform operating company doesn't hold your assets itself—a custodian company does—so your money is safe if the company has any 'problems'.

Share registry

Listed companies (and ETFs) can have millions of shareholders. That's a lot of administration to take on and records to keep, so companies and listed funds employ the services of a share registry to carry out administrative tasks.

Share registries are responsible for:

- managing shareholder communications, bank accounts for dividend payments and shareholders' contact details

- recording whether or not shareholders wish to reinvest their dividends automatically

- administering issues, which require a vote from the owners of a company (i.e. the shareholders), known as 'corporate actions'. Such issues could be voting on things like takeovers and acquisitions, share splits, buy-backs (where a company reduces the number of shares available and buys them back) and any other structural event that a company needs to have the shareholders agree on before proceeding.

You do not get to choose which registry you use, as the company or ETF you buy into selects this. You also receive details of dividend/ distribution payments from the share registry and you'll be able to log in to their portal to view your holdings if you have your own individual Holder Identification Number (HIN) (more on this in chapter 3).

Ticker / ticker code / ticker symbol

This is the code assigned to a company, ETF or any other listed instrument on an exchange. It's a unique reference for that holding. For example, the ticker code for the Commonwealth Bank of Australia is 'CBA' and the ticker code for JB Hi-Fi is 'JBH'. You'll find that some companies get creative for marketing purposes. In the United States there is an ETF that invests in industries associated with cannabis production and its ticker is 'WEED'.

Dollar-cost average

This is a common term used to indicate investing regular amounts over a period of time. It can also be referred to as dollar-cost averaging or 'DCA'. For example, if you purchased $500 worth of shares in a company each Friday for four weeks, the dollar-cost average might look like this:

- In week 1 the share price is $11.

- In week 2 the share price is $11.50.

- In week 3 the share price is $13.

- In week 4 the share price falls to $9.

The dollar-cost average of the total parcel of shares you now hold is the average of all four amounts, so your average buy price for $2000 worth of shares over those four weeks is $11.13.

This is a lot easier for your emotions than trying to time the market and buy when you think it's the right time to do so. What if you purchased only on the Friday when the price was $13 because you thought, 'Right, it's going to the moon. I'm jumping in, baby!' You would have paid a high price for your total parcel of shares. Granted, that you may have chosen the day that it was at $11, but using a DCA strategy for your investing removes you from the process and you'll receive the average share price for as long as you keep buying.

By the way, you already DCA with your employer's compulsory contributions into your superannuation account each month or quarter that the money is paid.

Bonds

Think of a bond as a loan that you give to a company or even the government! In return for your money, they promise to pay you back the principal amount you lent them after a certain period of time, plus interest payments along the way. Bonds are considered a safer type of investment compared to shares because you know exactly how much money you'll get back and when. They form part of the defensive portion of a portfolio. Corporate bonds may pay a slightly higher interest rate than a bank account when issued. This is to attract people to lend money to companies. Bonds can, however, be traded and at different times, due to market conditions, the traded value of the bond may be more or less than the 'face value'.

Okay. Now it's time to get you investing.

1

Know your 'why'

Glen

Why do you want to invest?

Our reasons for doing anything are often unknown even to ourselves. However, I want you to be consciously aware of why you're reading this book and why investing is something you're interested in.

Finding your 'why'

I regularly see soon-to-be investors seeking something quite specific. If you hadn't already thought of a 'why', this chapter could be a good prompt for you to start thinking and planning. One of the following reasons may resonate with you.

Get rich. Fast.

We have all heard the stories of people investing, becoming millionaires and having freedom in life without needing to work—well, so it seems. The chase for riches is usually the chase for freedom from your current life situation. Or, simply put, you don't like working and are sick of living week-to-week and not having opportunities to see the world, to enjoy the finer things in life and—for some—to have the status and clout of being 'rich'. You find yourself scrolling through Instagram, looking at nice clothes, watches, bags, cars and homes. You love the fantasy of being able to do whatever you want, whenever, without financial boundaries. You believe if only you had lots of money, most of your problems would go away.

Change your family's financial path

You may have grown up in a family or financial situation that offered limited opportunities for wealth. Or you may have been raised by a single parent trying to make the best of what was coming in. Perhaps your life growing up was fine but your family couldn't experience the extra little things that you saw other families enjoy, such as overseas holidays. Or maybe where you grew up was not a pleasant environment. You may be a first-generation Australian who immigrated as a young child and you now want to support your family. Regardless, you want your own kids and family not to have to go through what you went through. You want to change your family's financial path, starting with you.

Quit working asap

You hate your job. You live for Fridays and you hate Mondays. If you had more money and didn't rely on the income from your 9 to 5 life you would be so much happier. You could just sleep in every day, not have to worry about work and get some joy back in your life. Life has slipped past you and you feel like you're on a treadmill that you can't get off. Your financial commitments are too great and a career change is not on the cards because you'd have to go backwards before moving forwards. Making money from investing will enable you to quit that job sooner!

Increase your choices

You want to live 'life on your own terms'—or LOOT, as I like to call it. You don't want to live a 9 to 5 life. You want the option of working when you want, focusing on your side hustle or hobby, and being the true master of your own destiny. You want the choice to do things like taking an extended weekend away or spending time with your family and friends. Being untethered to social norms is a huge priority for you and investing will help you get there faster. You might be thinking, 'Isn't this everyone's goal?' Well, no. Some people enjoy the structure of a 9 to 5 role and life. They can leave work at work and enjoy non-work times. LOOT could be for solopreneurs or the free spirited!

Stop trading time for money

Passive income—that is, money appearing in your life without you having to trade an hour of your time working for it—is the eighth wonder of the world. You want to lean into investing because you understand that investing in shares is just about the only true form of passive income and you're all about that life. This is particularly relevant to you as you spend so much time at work wondering if you could ever earn more money on the side without having to trade the most limited thing on earth—time—for average money. You want more out of your life and money.

Provide for your kids

You have a family (or you're keen to start one) and want to give your kids the start to life that you didn't get. This could be a long-term investment account for a future home deposit, car or education.

This account could also be added to by family members rather than giving them wasteful toys or superficial presents for birthdays and Christmas. Investing for your kids will give you the tools to eventually hand them their investment account and start to educate them about investing, too. Or it might now be about providing your kids with their own investment account. You could be wanting to build wealth in your own name to give the kids the upbringing or opportunities you didn't have, such as extracurricular activities.

Plan for a dignified retirement

You may be later in your life stage and age and want to start looking at your retirement from the workforce, even if it's 10, 15 or 20 years away. Hundreds of dollars today can end up being thousands in the future. You may be at the stage where you own your house (or almost own it), you're financially established, you like your career, you don't want for much and you have spare money in your budget that needs to go to work. You want to invest for 'future you' to ensure you have a retirement not limited by money or opportunities.

What could be your 'why'?

Has what you just read helped you identify a reason for investing that stands out for you? There may be more than one. To be honest, the only one that may cause you issues is the 'get rich fast' goal because it's built off something that is superficial and fake. If you build your life on something that is based on consumption or consumerism, you'll run out of money and you'll end up being disappointed. In fact, if you were to invest just to become rich, you'd likely end up selling down your investments to spend on things that go down in value. Your 'why' is akin to finding the financial bedrock in your life, which I will explore later in this chapter.

What is money to you?

Is money good, bad, a blessing, a curse or something worthless made up by the government to control the world?

For at least 5000 years, money has been used in societies to represent an agreed value. It's a more practical and standardised way to exchange goods and services than a bartering system, where you would, for example, swap some sheep skin for a loaf of bread.

While the intrinsic value (total actual value of the material used) of a $100 note is probably not worth more than $1, our society has agreed that it represents an amount of $100 and is considered legal tender. It can be used to settle debts with the government and in exchange for goods and services. It is known as 'fiat currency', which means it's issued by a central or sovereign government and not backed by a commodity such as gold (though it used to be). The tin foil hats sometimes come out when people mention fiat currency and government control because the government can print more money (more than the supply of gold, which you can't make).

This is where inflation comes into play. If you had a finite amount of gold, its value would remain the same because there's no more available. But what if more gold was magically produced? Well, gold would then be worth less because there is more of it. Put simply, the same goes for your $100 note. If the government makes 10 more $100 notes and puts them into circulation, the value of that money reduces. This is where the great appeal of Bitcoin came from. It's limited and can't be reproduced. It's like digital gold. At the time of writing, Bitcoin can't settle any government debt ... so does it have real value? Not sure. Normal supply, demand and societal acceptance means we, the people, think it has value.

A quick note on inflation as this forms an important concept that you need to understand when investing.

If inflation isn't controlled well, or if there is corruption at play, there can be issues. Zimbabwe had to issue a 1 million Zimbabwe dollar note due to hyperinflation. *Yikes!*

When it comes to investing and money, inflation is the silent killer of value over time. When we invest, we take a risk to get a return on our money that is higher than the risk-free cash rate (think the no-risk interest earned from your bank account). Too often we don't think about inflation. But we definitely should. If inflation is 3 per cent and you receive 5 per cent from your bank account, the real return on your money each year is 2 per cent.

Now that you've learned about the simple history of money (even compared to a barter system), does this change what it means to you? What has your experience been in your life? In the first century, an influential man, Paul of Tarsus, suggested that the love of money is the root of all evil. Do you believe this? Have you seen this with your own eyes? Have you experienced oppression from those who have abused their power and wealth? Is money inherently evil or are people scumbags?

For me, and in my experience of life, money is neutral and it can be used for good or evil. Money doesn't have a mind, brain or personality. It is a tool. I have, however, noticed that money is a magnifier. If someone is a jerk and doesn't have much, they will be an even bigger jerk if they get a heap of money. This can be seen when Westerners visit developing nations on holidays. I'm disgusted by the way some people treat others when they have relatively more. But I have resolved it's the person, not the money itself, as some of the wealthiest people in the world have been able to use their money for good (think Bill and Melinda Gates Foundation).

A builder can use a hammer to build a beautiful house. But the same hammer can be used to destroy it by breaking windows. The hammer is the same. The problem is who is hanging onto it.

So money is a tool to me. What is it to you? I don't think there is a right or wrong answer here. I just want you to think about it and be aware.

Rich vs wealthy: acting rich will make you broke

I recently completed a TAFE course—a Certificate II in Maritime Operations. I did this because I enjoy boating and boaty things. I did it mainly out of personal interest and I had set my life and business up to be able to have two days off per week to do this course. You see, on the money and personal finance scene in Australia, I have a well-known name and podcast. I didn't want anyone in the class to know what I did because I just wanted to be another student. When someone in the class asked me what I did for work, I said I had an online media business and I was doing this course out of personal interest. I suddenly stood out like a sore thumb because many of the other students were there to progress their career in, or enter, the maritime industry. It was odd to have someone my age taking a course just out of interest.

It took about 10 seconds for a 23 year old in the small class of seven to google my name. He said in front of everyone, 'Hey Glen, are you rich?' To that I replied, 'No, I prefer wealthy'. Laughs ensued and my cover was up.

I share this story because I really think we need to position ourselves and our lives to become wealthy by working smart and slowly building wealth. Most people out there see being rich as a goal because, supposedly, it can make all your problems go away. There are countless stories in the history of humankind of wealth destroying people and families.

An organisation in the United States called the National Endowment for Financial Education tells us that 70 per cent of lottery winners go bankrupt within five years of winning. How wild is that! Not only do they lose their money, they go bankrupt. This means they have liabilities or bills they can no longer meet or pay.

A *Business Insider* article wrote about some lottery winners and what was one of the first things they did with their money. Let's have a laugh ... I mean look.

- *John & Linda Kutley (US$28.9m)* spent $200 000 to create a spray water park. These are like the open spaces in public parks where kids can run around and have a bit of fun with water.

- *Bob Erb (US$25m)* donated $1 million to an annual event to champion the cause of legalising marijuana. I'm not sure if Erb was his surname at birth (hehe).

- *Jonathan Varges (US$35m)* created Wrestlicious, a women's wrestling promotion (it's unknown how much it cost him). *Wrestlicious TakeDown* lasted one season.

- *Vivian Nicholson (~US$4m)* went shopping! Vivian won lotto in the UK in the 1960s and dedicated her life to buying nice clothes and an endless shopping spree. It did end, though, because by 2016 she had no money left.

While we don't know if all of these people ran out of money, we know one thing: the odds are not in your favour. The reason is when you don't earn money, you don't respect it. If you win the lottery tomorrow and spend the money on something that wasn't in your plans today, it can be a slippery slope. You see, if you did win US$35 million and spent $1 million on marijuana awareness, fun water parks or Wrestlicious, there is a high chance that these were not one-off splurges or planned investments (even though the public water park, for example, may have been a noble endeavour). Sure, $200 000 for a water fountain is a rounding error when it comes to US$28.9 million, but I wonder if the Kutleys had always wanted to build one.

Most people who win the lottery do one thing: they act rich. The type of rich we see in movies and on Instagram. This, my friends, is not reality. I wanted to take some time to talk about being 'rich' because it really shouldn't be the goal of anyone who is serious about building a life not limited by money. That sounds counterintuitive, but when you look at it, those lottery winners are limited by money: the money they won, the money they didn't earn. They are limited by a lack of systems and structure in their lives. They are limited by a lack of planning and vision for their lives. They are limited by a desire to spend and not to build and maintain wealth.

When we are strategic about building wealth and, more importantly, our life, we are measured and considered. This means that if money did come into our life, it would flow straight into our plan. If future wealth did all of a sudden appear in our lives from an inheritance or some other random occurrence, it shouldn't actually change the direction of our lives too much. If anything, you'd really want to at least do nothing for 6 to 12 months with any large windfall — with the exception of paying down debt.

I write this not only after reading stories of lottery winners, overnight celebrities or trust-fund kids blowing money overnight, but from my own learning and experience. I recently came into some money — we'll call it an inheritance-type sum — and you know what I did with it? Nothing. I'm clear on my purpose for investing in my own business, career, property and equities to the point that I don't want for anything and an amount of money that lands in my bank account doesn't lead me to run out and buy a new car or spend it on all the feel goods.

I say this not to brag but to show you that I have built a financially strong life, and I think you can too. I want you to build a life that you do not need money to escape from. Have money in your life to serve you. Build wealth to fund your planned life. Don't walk along aimlessly looking for wealth and money to create your life.

Let's have a look at some of the differences between being rich and being wealthy.

If you are rich — or act rich — you may have some or all of the following attributes:

- You have a high income.

- You spend money on depreciating assets.

- You care about appearances.

- You want instant gratification.

- You work for money.

Now, some of these can be true if you're not 'rich'. For example, you may have high self-confidence, which may be one of the 20 signs that you're a narcissist when you're not. But picture the previous list if you were earning more than $180 000 per year and didn't have much to your name.

If you're wealthy, you may have some or all of the following attributes:

- You have a high net worth (total of all assets less all liabilities).

- You spend money on appreciating assets.

- You don't care about appearances.

- You have strong discipline and you can delay gratification.

- You make your money work for you.

The good news is that as investors, we manage our money well because it grows slowly and is generally earned, not won. You'll always appreciate what you have earned and built more than what has been given to you.

How do you think you're acting right now? Regardless of your income or assets, you can act rich or wealthy. I've come across hundreds of people who are on average Australian salaries and are living well beyond their means, essentially acting rich or not acting their income. Around 75 per cent of the *this is money* podcast community, when surveyed, do not have consumer debt. This is a great start and a sign that you're not acting rich. If in doubt, ask your friends and family.

Think about ways you may be acting rich and how you can stop this.

A 3-point plan for managing money

Another piece to your investing preparation is understanding how you should manage your money. My belief, for my own life, is pretty simple. I only do three things with this tool that I have:

1. I live on less than I earn.

2. I give generously.

3. I invest the rest.

This is my 3-point plan. Because I have these principles locked in, my own 'why I invest' is supported and allows me to invest after I have been financially generous.

If you don't have a 3-point 'why' statement, you can adopt mine using the things you value. Let's look at what each of the points means.

Live on less than you earn

I have resolved, after several years in my early 20s of not making good financial progress, that I will not consume more than I earn. This means I have no consumer debt. I even save up and pay cash for cars. I only borrow money for buying residential real estate. I have a solid spending plan in place and an emergency fund as a back-up and both these things slow me down with regard to making unnecessary purchases.

Be a generous giver

You can't give anything away because it always comes back. I've resolved that financial generosity is also a core part of my life. We live in such a privileged country that has, on balance, great schools, healthcare and a relatively high standard of living. I reckon because

I'm in a good position I can give to those less fortunate and this also does slow me down (on purpose) with splurging on luxuries and building wealth. I'm okay with having a smaller investment account or less 'stuff' because I've been generous along the way (and I'll still be fine).

Invest the rest

Part of my investing strategy is to park money for the future — I'll touch on this in chapter 2. But basically, I invest whatever is left over. This could be in real estate or equities. I don't believe this needs to be too prescriptive as things could change. I might not buy a property for a few years but invest heavily in ETFs.

Make your own 3-point plan

Can you make your own 3-point plan for your money that you can really live and breathe, repeat to others without thinking and turn into a living mantra for your financial life? Remember: this will need to be broad and futureproof. I haven't changed mine in more than 10 years. That's not to say things can't change, but once you really understand what money is and work through your 'why' you'll be able to develop this. If you have a spouse or partner I'd recommend you both have a 3-point plan for your household. Remember to include investing in your three points wherever it suits you best.

Here are some other examples that might get you thinking:

- Invest in experiences over things.

- Save for the future, but don't forget to enjoy today.

- Diversify investments to minimise risk.

- Always be learning and growing.

- Avoid consumer debt at all costs.

- Have at least two income streams at all times.

- Invest in health as a priority.

- Practise mindful spending, not impulsive buying.

- Always have at least three months of emergency savings.

- Live in the now but always plan for the future.

- Focus on long-term gains rather than short-term pleasures.

- Maintain a healthy work–life balance that is family centric.

- Invest in relationships as much as in shares.

- Embrace minimalism when investing

... or another point that resonates with you and your goals.

Investing in action

1. What could your starter 3-point plan be?

2. What three points do you want guiding how you manage your money? Think about big and broad themes you want to focus on.

My sound financial house

Okay, I'm sorry but I can't speak about investing without talking about my sound financial house! While I explained this in detail in my previous books, it would be remiss of me not to mention it in relation to investing. You see, when it comes to investing in shares, it's even more important to do things in the right order because shares are liquid and can be easily sold down.

If you purchased an investment property and then a couple of years later you were a bit short on money to pay your expenses or you needed an extra $1000 for an emergency, you wouldn't sell the property to cover this. That's not practical. Instead, you might stop going out, not go to that concert next month or really tighten things up to get through the bump. But if you had a portfolio of $10 000 worth of investments in a couple of ETFs, it would be really easy to just log in and sell down $1000 to cover your unexpected expense. But should you? Figure 1.1 illustrates the downside of doing this.

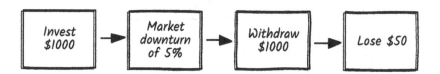

Figure 1.1: how to lose money when investing in shares or ETFs

If your foundations are not in place, the 'once-off' sell-down of shares can become a habit and then, if you sold down when the market wasn't strong, you'd actually lose money. A couple of things can happen here. Your poor financial habits won't get resolved and your financial situation can compound negatively.

If you had an emergency fund and a solid spending plan before you started investing, this would not be an issue because you'd have built your financial house on strong foundations. That's what a sound financial house does for you. To see what my sound financial house looks like, check out figure 1.2.

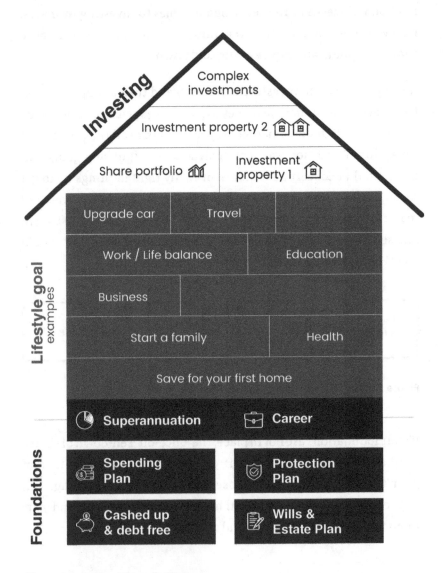

Figure 1.2: a sound financial house

Common money-management pitfalls

I became a contrarian after seeing too many people getting money stuff wrong! Like gloating over having a brand new car financed like mad with insane interest rates and seven years to pay it off. Or borrowing money to travel overseas and returning with a double-digit credit card debt. Or choking up the weekly cash flow just because they were feeling spendy (something I battle with myself).

There are so many aspects to how we choose to spend, manage and invest our money. Much of it is simply due to good marketing. Some could be the result of someone we know saying, 'Hey, this thing over here has worked for me — you should do it too!' Far too often I've seen my clients, or listeners of my podcast, get tangled in the weeds of money management instead of building a strong foundation like my sound financial house. I guess it happens when most of us aren't brought up having real conversations about money with our family or friends.

I'd encourage you to really nail what you think about money management because life is fluid and things change. It's important that you want your money to stay invested once it's invested and not withdrawn to be used for day-to-day life.

Being a contrarian in the personal finance space can be helpful when you're talking to the media to get that headline for some exposure on a personal level. But it can be hard because you are going against the grain, which can make you feel like the crazy one in the room.

There are some common pitfalls I see people getting stuck in when managing their personal finances. A few of these follow, along with my contrarian view and rationale for each one. See what you think. Do you agree or disagree with me? It's totally fine if you disagree.

Debt consolidation

A popular term in money land is debt consolidation. What is it? Well, the theory is that if you have multiple debts (cars, personal loans, credit cards) with various interest rates and monthly payments, you consolidate them into one debt and just pay that one debt down.

My contrarian view: you're not fixing the problem — you're just moving the debt. The problem is that you overspend. Get a spending plan and pay the debt off.

Zero-based budgeting

This is akin to a traditional budget where you allocate very specific amounts from your pay to exact categories (down to the cent!). For example, each time you are paid, each dollar is given a specific job and anything left over is targeted at saving or investing. This approach requires a very close eye and a lot of time reviewing expenses. Imagine trying to achieve a specific target of $0.00 in your account after you've allocated money to your expenses!

My contrarian view: money needs to breathe and flow with your life. Expenses go up and down, and trying to be specific to the dollar can make it exhausting to manage. This is why I like to have a spending plan that allocates money each pay into accounts for specific purposes using rounded-up figures. Give it a few pay cycles and you'll see these accounts build up. It takes a whole lot of pressure off non-engineer type people, who need to ensure they have money ready when they need it. If an expense increases, you can increase the amount you are putting away for that expense. There might be $100 left over after all of your expenses are paid, or $10. The focus is more on having enough money there for your needs when they arise. We want our engineers to design things to the millimetre, and they're welcome to run their money like this too, but the rest of us can't. ☺

Credit cards

Many 'money people' say that a credit card is a great tool because it allows you to use other people's (the bank's) money without paying interest for the month while your own money can sit in an account receiving interest.

My contrarian view: many people suck at managing money and have no self-control, so paying the debt off within the interest-free period often doesn't happen. If this does work on paper, there is a high chance that people will overspend on credit, negating the whole strategy. There is less pain when you spend on credit as opposed to your own money. Credit cards only exist because, on balance, they make money from people overspending. I choose not to use credit cards for day-to-day expenses. I like to keep my money life simple. 'Doing it for the points' is also a strategy that seldom works for many as the potential for overspending and being sloppy means you actually buy the points with the overspent money. The risk with this overspending is you end up with debt that you struggle to pay off ... and the cycle starts again and continues.

Paying down debt

If you receive a bonus or come into some money, even $1000, and you have debt, many 'money people' will say that you should pay this straight onto your buy-now-pay-later account, personal loan or credit card. You didn't expect the money anyway and you need to get out of debt! Debt is your biggest financial problem at the moment.

My contrarian view: don't pay down the debt. Put this money into a starter emergency fund, out of sight and out of mind. You need to ensure that you have some money behind you in case you find yourself in a financial pickle. Debt is not your biggest problem — your spending behaviour is. This is the start of a behavioural change for those who are stuck in the debt cycle. If something bad happens, you don't want more debt so that $1000 will come in very handy.

Investing in shares as soon as you can

The sooner you start, the more money you will have down the track. Compounding interest (and compounding dividend reinvestment) is the true magic of money. These statements can't be more true. I do agree with these; however ...

My contrarian view: I'd rather you devote time and energy to building your career before you worry about putting all your money away for the future, even if this means you stay cash heavy until you've finished your education, training or get established into your career. Your ability to earn money from your job will outpace any dividends you receive or investment capital you allocate. (I'll talk about this in chapter 2.) I believe your career is the first investment you should make. I understand it can be helpful to put smaller amounts into investing apps while you build your career to stay focused and engaged with investing, but your career still needs to come first. If you're not happy with your current job or career, I'd suggest working on that asap.

Investing in quality companies only

It's common to hear that it's important to invest in quality companies that have a strong track record, future earnings growth and a moat around them. Spend time researching these companies before you invest in them.

My contrarian view: well, this is an investing book, so I needed a view on this. I don't buy single stocks with more than 10 per cent of my portfolio. Who has time to read and understand financial data and then form a view? Not me. With the availability of ETFs nowadays there is no reason to not diversify. They say 'don't put money in the bank—buy the bank'. Don't buy the bank—buy all of them and another few hundred companies in one go. This will stop FOMO when you see other single companies that you don't own doing better than the ones you own. Good investing is more about solid behaviour than what you invest in, on balance (when it comes to individual companies vs broad-based ETFs).

O O O

These contrarian views have served me well over my life. I want you to think about any views you have about money and where they may have come from. ☺

While these examples speak to personal finance management, the underlying framework is based on my sitting down face-to-face with hundreds of people over the years helping them with their money—this, coupled with hearing thousands of podcast listeners say that they turned their financial lives around by following my approaches.

The thing that has shaped my contrarian views—which leads partly into knowing my 'why' when it comes to investing—is behaviour.

Do you have a view? Is it different from mine?

What is your financial bedrock?

By implementing what I've shared in this chapter, you've essentially built your financial bedrock. Your 'why', your belief about what money is and the 3-point plan will guide how you think money should be managed and invested. They come together to form a pyramid like the one in figure 1.3 (overleaf). Each element is connected and builds on the others.

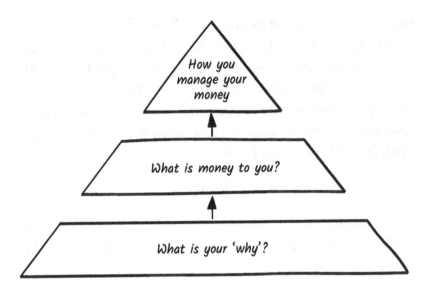

Figure 1.3: your financial bedrock

So how does yours look?

Something worth noting is that you're likely an investor already! If you are an employee, on top of your earnings your employer will be paying retirement savings into your superannuation. This money is invested into the share market and various other assets on your behalf. It's a tax-effective environment (which is something we will get to in chapter 3). This is your money, even though it may not feel like it, because you didn't physically transfer it from your bank account over to the investment account. It can provide some solace if you are itching to get invested but you are not 100 per cent ready because you need to work on your 'why' a bit more before you start allocating your own after-tax dollars to investing.

Superannuation is in place because governments want to ensure that there is some type of compulsory retirement savings for citizens so when they retire from the workforce there is less of a reliance on social security. The thing is, on balance, most humans consume what they have and live without thinking long term. Working through your 'why' and the following chapter on behaviours will help you control your own money, and in turn, your financial future.

You are an investor already, but I hope I've enabled you to understand your 'why', or as Oprah said, to find 'your truth'! This will be different for everyone — and that's how it should be.

Start with this ...

There's plenty to consider for your own situation. Have a think about:

* Your 'why': Why are you investing? What's driving you?

* What money is to you. If you have 'enough' money, what does your life look like?

* How you think money should be managed. What are the three principles that guide your money and investing?

* Whether you've fallen into any financial management traps. What behaviours need to stop, and what changes need to be made?

* For a more in-depth explanation of my sound financial house, follow the QR code on page 204 to see an explainer video.

2

Think and act like an investor

Glen

I am your constant companion. I am your greatest helper or heaviest burden. I will push you onward or drag you down to failure. I am completely at your command. Half the things you do you might as well turn over to me, and I will be able to do them quickly and correctly. I am easily managed — you must merely be firm with me. Show me exactly how you want something done, and after a few lessons I will do it automatically. I am the servant of all great people; and alas, of all failures as well. Those who are great, I have made great. Those who are failures, I have made failures.

I am not a machine, though, I work with all the precision of a machine plus the intelligence of a man. You may run me for a profit or run me for ruin — it makes no difference to me. Take me, train me, be firm with me, and I will place the world at your feet. Be easy with me and I will destroy you.

Who am I?

(To find the answer to this riddle, please see the end of the chapter.)

It's not known who wrote this but I believe it's one of the most powerful riddles I've ever read. What if you read it with money management at the forefront of your mind?

Control your money, control your future

Money management can be hard, but it doesn't have to be.

I reckon for the first handful of my adult years, I was a financial trainwreck. Most of us were never taught how to handle and manage money and as you enter adulthood you don't have much anyway so it's a lose-lose situation — particularly with the barrage of marketing in our daily feeds; cafe and social culture; and many of our friends getting engaged, married and having kids in their 20s. Not to mention the cost of rent, needing a decent car to get around in and potentially study fees. I mean, after all that if you're saving money you're doing something right! You are not the norm, so well done!

Everyone else needs to really nail money management. If you don't, there's no point in investing because chances are you'll be using consumer debt to invest, which makes no sense. Or your lack of managing money well will find you having to sell down your investments to fund other things in your life, which defeats the purpose of investing to start with.

To this day, I'm not great at saving money. I'm a spender by nature and I've recently received a diagnosis of ADHD, which I'm now getting treated for. But thankfully I was self-aware enough to look at my own habits and behaviours and develop a system that would protect me and my financial future. You see, I can be very impulsive and this can cause great financial waste. *Yikes.* However, because I have a rock-solid system in place, I grow money year-on-year without spending it and still live my best life!

I want to look at two high-level behavioural structures that you can think about when it comes to managing yourself and your money. I promise you: if you can't control the person in your mirror (and your money!), you will not be a ~~good~~ great investor.

Behavioural structure 1: The bottom-up budget

In business, a bottom-up budget basically works out what you need to spend to get the doors open. Then you can look at revenue targets to match and then make a profit above the expenses. When you translate this model to your personal life you essentially pay your expenses first and give, save or invest whatever is left.

I run a bottom-up budget in my life and I also teach this in the free online course I run, 'The Glen James Spending Plan'. The reason I do and teach this is because I want to have (and I'm sure you do too) a life that I can live without restrictions and in relative comfort. Everyone has expenses, whether they be a mortgage repayment, rent, electricity, transportation costs, children, sport or medical requirements ...

Simply put, because everyone has these expenses in their life, we get to a number where we find out 'this is what it costs me to wake up each morning'. We hope there will be leftover money once we work out how much it costs us to wake up of a morning. Then we can carve up that money for short-term savings, long-term savings and then investing for the future.

The other very important reason I teach money management this way is many people I teach come to me without a plan and not being able to save money. They may live week-to-week and not have a good financial foundation, even though they have a great income. Because money management and investing is all about behaviours, to get a great outcome you can't start cold turkey by taking away everything from someone's life and devoting 20 per cent of their income to investing. You need to first get them on a system that works for them where they can start to see some small wins early on. If you had a morning coffee every day and then tomorrow you were not allowed to do this anymore, I dare say you wouldn't stick to the new system. It's too hard too early on.

Figure 2.1 depicts what a bottom-up budget approach might look like.

This is not to say that we should spend whatever we want and then invest. But it's a way to get you started. After that you can optimise each budget line item and add more money to investing! You will get to the point where you can ask yourself, 'Do I need 15 subscriptions or am I happy to have one and put the money I was spending on multiple subscriptions into my future by investing?'

When starting on my bottom-up approach, I'd suggest following the steps shown in figure 2.2.

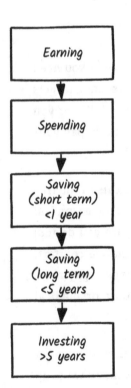

Figure 2.1: my bottom-up approach to investing

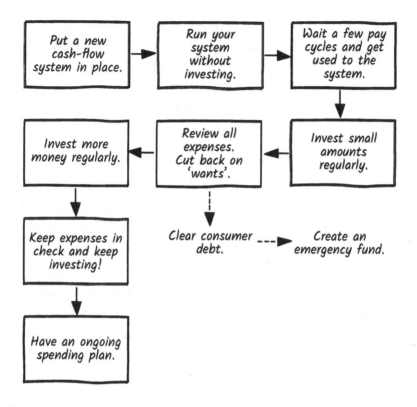

Figure 2.2: setting up your bottom-up approach

Investing small amounts

I don't mind people investing small amounts regularly if they are new to a system, still have consumer debt or do not have an emergency fund. This small amount will keep you engaged and learning. It will help if you have a bit of FOMO. But you can't be under the illusion that you don't have to get out of debt, or have an emergency fund, or need to focus on using and sticking to your new money system.

I reckon if you're new to this or working on your foundations and still want to invest a small amount, maybe 1 per cent per year of your gross income, go for it! Table 2.1 (overleaf) gives you some estimates.

Table 2.1: how much 1% of your income amounts to

Income	1% per year
$50 000	$500 (or $41 per month)
$70 000	$700 (or $58 per month)
$80 000	$800 (or $66 per month)
$90 000	$900 (or $75 per month)

I cannot stress enough that these small amounts are only to get you interested, focused and learning about investing—and they can be invested with investing apps. While you're getting your new system up and running, getting out of debt or creating an emergency fund, do not fear: you are still an investor because you are receiving regular monthly superannuation contributions from your employer for future you. Of course, you do not have to invest small amounts if you don't want to. You may want to wait until you have your sound financial house in order. But the sooner you are out of consumer debt and have an emergency fund to fall back on, the better it will feel and the more you can fully lean into investing!

What's the difference between saving and investing?

Short-term savings refers to things like weekends away, new furniture and whitegoods. These might be small enough to save for over 12 months or less, but do not include ongoing planned larger bills like insurances or car registration. These are generally one-off expenses—like a new mattress or fridge—not annual recurring expenses.

Long-term savings are for big holidays, weddings, car upgrades, family planning or building up a war chest in order to be cash heavy to start your own business.

You should keep short- and long-term savings in a dedicated online savings account earning interest, or in a separate offset account.

Investing refers to any money that isn't spoken for in your life that needs to go to work to build your financial future. You could contribute more to superannuation (pre- or post-tax), buy property or invest in shares / ETFs in your own name.

Behavioural structure 2: The top-down budget

In business, this structure focuses firstly on top-line revenue and then appropriates that revenue to set expenses linked to certain department budgets — the opposite of a bottom-up budget. When translating this to your personal life, it's like giving, saving and investing first, and covering your expenses with whatever is left. It looks a bit like figure 2.3.

With this approach, you might say, 'Every time I get paid, the first thing I'm doing is putting 10 to 20 per cent into saving/investing and then I will spend the remaining 80 per cent on all other living expenses'. You lock up money to invest for the future first.

While this is great in theory, is very militant and would ensure you are living well within

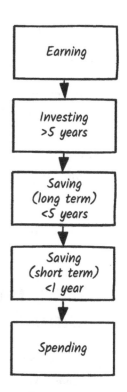

Figure 2.3: the top-down approach to investing

your means, I've only seen this system work for the following types of people:

- Those who have done this since they had their first job in school or leaving school. The behaviours and habits are so set that they have built their life around this

- Those who are extremely frugal and are skilled at living in a very cost-conscious way

- Those who want to pursue an aggressive form of 'FIRE' (Financial Independence, Retire Early)

- Those who are engineers and the like (hi!).

While you will ensure you amass great wealth as a priority using this approach, I will also caution you that sometimes you can lose sight of the now: miss out on opportunities, not enjoy what you work so hard for and maybe even piss off some loved ones in your life because you come across as 'tight'. And hey, maybe you do need to loosen up and enjoy life a little!

I've always tried to live and teach an approach where you have two eyes, so use them both: one eye on the now and one on the future.

What money system should you use?

The short answer is always 'whatever works for you and gives you proven results'. I will say, for the thousands of people who have completed The Glen James Spending Plan after not having a system for managing money in place — and overspending and finding themselves in a financial mess without savings — following my bottom-up approach has always worked well. This is because habits and behaviours are more important than anything else when it comes to personal finance and investing. Our money habits and behaviours sometimes need to change and, for the best results, they ideally need to change slowly so we don't notice the changes. These habits and behaviours are crucial not only for our day-to-day spending and saving habits, but also for committing actual money to investing, which I will get into shortly.

You just need to know one thing: poor money management and building a strong financial future cannot exist together. Pick one. I choose the latter. There is honestly no point investing in shares if you don't manage your money well, as depicted in figure 2.4.

Figure 2.4: poor money management and building a strong financial future can't exist together

How to approach investing

You may be very clear on your 'why' when it comes to why you want to invest. That's great. You need this as an overarching focal point or embedded purpose for when things get tough in your life (they will), when distractions or emergencies happen (they will) or if you get bored (you will). Your 'why' will tether you to your future goals. But where does that leave investing when such things happen? After reading chapter 1 you'll know what your financial bedrock is made up of: your 'why', your belief about what money is and a 3-point plan. Let's focus on investing as part of your 3-point plan.

What is your philosophy around money that has been committed to your investing account? You might not have thought about this yet, so I'll tell you mine.

I have a slightly different view from many other people when it comes to investing. You see, I don't invest to 'make money'. Of course all investments should make money—that's granted. My mindset when it comes to investing is to park money that I do not need today where it can grow for the long term. It needs to grow at a higher rate than inflation and cash, it needs to be diversified and it needs to be simple.

I truly believe that the best investment you will ever make is in yourself and your career, as this gives you the ability to earn an income. The income you earn creates cash flow for living here and now; and the more you earn, the more you can be investing. Your career and life should be where most of your focus goes when it comes to wealth generation. Whether you're progressing your employment or creating a business, the true exchange of your energy for dollars is where it's at. Then you can transfer and park some of this human capital (as much as you can) into your investment account to grow for the future. This takes the pressure off your investments because you aren't racing to have your day-to-day needs covered by investment returns. Diversity is key! A lot of people believe having a large investment account is the answer to all their problems. It really isn't.

Parking money and letting it grow at a reasonable rate above inflation and the risk-averse option of having money in a bank account means you don't need to take excessive investing risks. Having a bigger pile of money sooner will not solve all your problems. Trust me, I tried to have money solve my problems and even when the money grew the problems didn't go away.

Let me illustrate why 'investing' shouldn't be the cornerstone of your wealth-creation strategy.

Let's say you have a small investing portfolio of $20 000. Look at table 2.2 to see what some hypothetical annual returns could be if your investment has a successful year. You'll see in the one-year return results, the returns aren't mind-blowing. You won't be retiring to the Bahamas tomorrow with that cash. However, when paired with a strong income, diversity of investments like superannuation *and* investing, you can build wealth in a steady and sustainable way.

Table 2.2: hypothetical annual returns for an investing portfolio of $20 000

Asset class	Characteristics	Considered risk	Value	One-year return
Cash	Capital secure, liquid, interest income, inflation will eat value over time	Low	$20 000	5% or $1000
ETF IOZ Top 200 Australian companies	Capital fluctuates, liquid, diversified, dividend income	Medium	$20 000	8% or $1600
Single listed company (top 200)	Capital fluctuates, liquid, dividend income, not diversified	High	$20 000	11% or $2200
Startup company	Capital not guaranteed, illiquid, dividend not guaranteed, no diversification	Extreme	$20 000	50% or $10 000

I want to use figure 2.5 (overleaf) to demonstrate a few things:

- Most of the time, most people would ideally like to have the lion's share of their wealth in the medium/medium-high risk profile band, illustrated with the circle in figure 2.5.

- It's exciting to hear about and invest in startup companies as many have had fantastic returns. However, for all the unicorns you hear of, there are hundreds each year that fail and you never hear about them.

- You do not — I repeat, *do not* — want more than 5 to 10 per cent of your portfolio sitting in the extreme risk section of a risk table. Maybe even under 5 per cent. This is risk tolerance and financial situation specific.

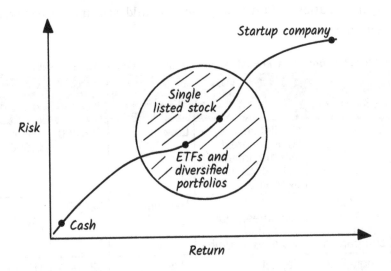

Figure 2.5: the risk and return partnership: the less risk, the less potential reward, but you'll also see less volatility. The greater the risk, the greater the potential reward, but success isn't always guaranteed.

Back to your employment income and why it's important when it comes to investing. If you wanted to grow your investment portfolio by $10 000 in one year, for someone who has less than $100 000 invested, their employment will be the best shot at doing this.

Why? Let's look at Mia in figure 2.6 as an example. Knowing that investment returns won't sky-rocket from the $20 000 Mia has invested, her greatest source of income is from her employment.

I'd want Mia focusing on protecting and building that, rather than striving to make her investments work harder at this stage—that will happen in time.

Mia is:
- 28 years old
- $20 000 invested
- Well into career
- Earns $70 000
- Happy in her line of work (Marketing team member)

Figure 2.6: building Mia's employment income and investment returns: utilising the strength of her income is the best first step as it gives investments time to grow.

If Mia was feeling like risking the biscuit and becoming the day trader of her dreams, she could dive deep into investing in shares to create passive income. Imagine her hustle: digging deep into complex investments for maximum returns. But it would be far less risky for Mia to leave her $20 000 in a diversified 'medium risk' portfolio and see what she can do with her career to get a $10 000 pay rise. That pay rise would be a whole lot easier to achieve by meeting with her boss than by risking her cash in speculative investments and pushing hard for epic returns.

The thing is, with this mindset there is far less risk for Mia's overall situation by growing her employment income as opposed to having her whole portfolio sitting in a potentially extreme risk category. No thanks!

Plus, that $10 000 pay rise is like a risk-free annuity. It will keep showing up each year and her investment portfolio doesn't need to be anywhere near the extreme risk category. I've never seen anyone getting a pay decrease in their line of work unless there is a career pivot.

You might say, 'Well, income is taxed, so it doesn't count as wealth creation'. I would say, 'So is investment income'.

Think of it this way: when you work, you trade your time for money. If Mia is on $35 per hour, after tax she's getting $27. If she invested just one hour (i.e. $27) per week at an 8 per cent return, after inflation of 3 per cent, in 20 years that $27 would be worth just under $70 (that's in today's dollars!). So with a long-term investing view in mind, she is on $70 an hour if she invests and keeps it invested.

Don't approach investing with the view that this one avenue — this *one* investing road — will change your life forever. The wealthiest people I know are living off diversified streams of income — some active, some passive. Investing does come into it, but it isn't the only source of wealth.

I need you to start thinking about your income and employment when it comes to investing. You can't segment financial parts of your life — they are all connected. Remember: don't focus on something (like investing) to solve all your problems, because it seldom will. Focus on your life and career and build/park excess money (wealth) for the long term.

It's important to look at investing through this lens as you build your life, career and portfolio. The truth is, the best return you'll get from your portfolio, particularly when it's less than $100 000, is the capital you put in yourself — that is, by transferring your human capital to be invested for the future.

Take a look at table 2.3 and the approximate 'return' of various portfolios if you add $100 per week. This is important to understand so that you focus more on your savings rate than the perfect investment and trying to get huge gains by taking extreme risks.

Table 2.3: portfolio returns based on adding $100 per week

Portfolio balance	Return of $100 per week added
$20 000	26.00%
$35 000	14.85%
$50 000	10.00%
$70 000	7.43%
$100 000	5.20%

Want a 26 per cent per annum return on your $20 000 portfolio? Just add $5200 of your own money!

Now don't @ me for not being down to the cents with compounding over the year. I want you to learn big-picture concepts from this table.

Investing in action

Write down the sources of income in your life that are adding to your overall wealth position. Consider your employment, income from side hustles or second jobs, your superannuation, investing and any other part of your life that's creating income.

When investing behaviours fail

If you want a dopamine hit, go to the casino. Investing is, and should be, boring. Amassing wealth will not solve all your problems, so don't bother trying. Seriously, if you are investing just to get rich so life will be easier, stop now.

Let's play this out. If you had some spare money to invest to build wealth so you can retire early, there is little (to no) chance of this happening within the next five years. This is because most of the returns needed to build a portfolio are going to be from the capital (savings) that you invest.

You'd likely need to build a portfolio of at least $500 000. This is also not realistic if you want to replace your income, but it's a good start for my illustration.

Being conservative, you'd need to save at least $6400 per month for five years to get to $500 000. You would also need a guaranteed return of 10 per cent to do this. (You'd likely actually need more than this per month as this doesn't account for taxes on income each year. Most of us don't have a spare $6400 to invest per month! Good problem to have though.)

My point is, if you could 'retire' and have no financial problems in five years' time after having accrued a portfolio to live off, you would have to endure another five years of hoping to invest as a means to escape your 9 to 5 working, forever-bill-paying life to get there. This means you should really try to work on yourself and your life as a priority, because if you endure five more years of hell while you save and invest you will likely end up being the same person you are now with the money not having solved your problems.

Am I guilty of being a realist? Yes.

Am I saying don't bother investing and building wealth? No.

What I'm getting at is that part of my mindset when it comes to investing is that I'm literally parking money that I don't need now to grow for future me. This money grows at a rate higher than the cash rate and inflation (which are the true benchmarks to outperform). It takes all the pressure off me wanting to make lots of money in the short term thinking it will solve my problems. I need to ensure I'm living on less than I earn, and saving (investing) the rest. I am happy with my life and income and want to focus on living, not investing. Investing happens in the background.

The reason it is crucial to have this investor mindset is because:

- you too will see investing as parking money for the long term

- you could comfortably invest in broad-based ETFs/index funds and see decent performance without unnecessary risk

- you will be less likely to buy and sell your ETFs all the time, wanting to get the 'best portfolio'

- you will be less likely to do dumb things like invest larger amounts in speculative investments

- it will help you put your investing on autopilot for most of the time: a set-and-forget strategy.

I personally don't worry about targeted returns and financial projections when investing. My mindset is to just build wealth in a way that has reasonable risk and will outperform cash and inflation. Anything above that means I'm ahead of the curve. Targeted returns may be useful if you want to save for something over, say, 10 years (e.g. kids' education or a specific time-bound goal) because they can help you determine how much you need to put in each month. But, on balance, the mindset I'm talking about is for building long-term wealth for future you.

The other reason this mindset is beneficial is that it helps you control the number-one investment asset: you. Controlling yourself and being happy with your lot in life will make you a better investor. Don't look for external things to make you content and happy. These simple statements are seldom written in investing books because those books assume everyone is well controlled and behaved, and lives in a perfect world. The thing is, investing and building wealth is easy and straightforward — people are not. And, we do not live in a perfect world.

Control the person in your mirror and control your financial future. If you want excitement, don't look for it from investing.

Before I was diagnosed with depression and anxiety, and subsequently medicated, I was not the best version of me. In fact, I would look for external things to make me feel better and in control of my future. I would take big investing risks and chop and change all the time. I didn't end up making great investment progress as I would always sell down my portfolio to buy things and just kept going around in circles. This, coupled with not being happy with my work and career, made for one big mess. I know this isn't a problem for everyone, but my situation would resonate with a lot of people.

My question is, are you happy with your career and life? Are you trying to escape it by getting wealthy fast? If you answered no to the first question, I would implore you to focus on 'you' before you start committing big amounts of money to investing. Speak with your GP if you do not feel settled, are always in a bad mood or have trouble sleeping. Good mental health and building wealth go hand-in-hand.

The two big traps of investing behaviour

Humans are fickle and unpredictable. We need to look at the two biggest behavioural finance traps that I believe you can fall into, if you're not careful, as an investor: hype and confirmation bias.

Hype

The rise and fall of the value of Bitcoin (or any cryptocurrency) is strongly correlated with the amount of hype associated with the asset, either online or in real life. Funny that, isn't it?

The more people were talking about Bitcoin, the higher the price became. When a tipping point came and some of the hype wore off, fewer people were suddenly wanting to buy Bitcoin. With fewer people wanting to buy and the same supply in the market, the price fell.

We have seen these cycles come and go over the years with Bitcoin. The reason it's a good illustration of hype is that it has arguably no intrinsic value. It's worth what someone is prepared to pay for it.

Hype and FOMO can make us do dumb things. With behavioural finance, this is what's known as 'herding'—or a herding bias or mentality—meaning people follow what others are doing without thinking about their own situation and analysis or conducting their own due diligence. I believe herding when investing comes from either or all of the following:

- Being lazy and thinking because others are doing it, it must be okay.

- A deep sense of FOMO on massive returns.

- Not having your own strategy in place and sticking to it.

It's funny that people will not 'herd' to a broad-based index of the top 500 companies in the US market or the top 200 companies in Australia. It only really occurs when there is the chance to strike gold and make lots of money fast. For every cryptocurrency or unicorn company that has gone to the moon, there are thousands of investments that have had hype and investors ended up without a cent.

Just think, if you did put $500 into Bitcoin and it went to the moon and you gained 300 per cent in 2 months ... you'd end up with an extra $1500. While this is nice and you'd take it, it won't change your life. You've had a dopamine hit. For it to really change your life, you'd want to have put all of your money in it ... and that's just not wise at all.

There is a difference between a speculative investment opportunity and a herding mentality. Are you doing something because everyone else is and it's talked about everywhere and seems to make people millions of dollars? Or is it an opportunity that has come your way that interests you and you are keen to put a small percentage of your portfolio into the opportunity? I'm more of a fan of the latter. However, I never put more than 5 to 10 per cent of my portfolio in highly speculative investments because the odds are not in my favour.

To protect yourself against herding behaviour:

- know that if everyone is talking about it, it's probably too late to invest in it successfully

- be confident that your strategy works for you and that it's a long-term play

- try to remove yourself from manually investing month-on-month — use automation instead

- understand some big wins on small amounts will not change your life

- know that it's real and irrational.

I used Bitcoin as an example, but the truth is it can happen with listed companies too. A million years ago (2000s) when the dot-com bubble was expanding, people were buying shares in companies that had no value, no income and no real plan. The values just kept increasing because the demand was increasing. If a listed company was involved with the internet, that was enough for people to jump into investing in it, without question. Some of these businesses succeeded, some did not. Some investors lucked out. Don't be fooled into thinking because this was a quarter of a century ago that it won't happen again. Time changes but human nature does not.

How do you remove hype from your investing life? Be rock solid with your strategy (buy and hold broad-based ETFs) and if you want to dip your toe in, be very strict and only put a small percentage of your money into such endeavours.

Confirmation bias

When someone asks you which dentist they should go to (or about any other service), you say, 'You gotta see Lacey! She is the best dentist ever! OMG!' The thing is, you've had a good experience with her, she has looked after you and is reasonably priced. Does that mean she is actually the best dentist? No. How can you know with certainty? You only think she is the best because you have a bias towards this particular dentist because of your familiarity and your own positive experience.

The same can happen with investing. For example, you bank with a big four bank and you figure you may as well own some of its shares because it has been a good bank for you. Or you shop at a large supermarket and figure you should buy shares in it because you're a loyal customer and you shop there. The thing is, you can't base your investing decisions and strategy on feelings or irrational biases. These need to be separate — always. What if the bank you use has the best app and you love using it, but the bank you have chosen to invest in has been a dog for many years ... and if only you'd chosen another bank you would have gotten a higher return.

How do I remove confirmation bias? I do this by only investing in broad-based indexes. I also understand that I can't possibly know everything and I'm okay with that.

What have I resolved about investing behaviour?

I've come to realise that I am nothing, I know nothing and if I start to think I am anything more than a podcaster and a guy who likes his boat, I do dumb things and it costs me. Another law of the universe right behind the law of gravity is that if you get desperate, you end up broke — I added figure 2.7 just to give you a visual of this. You're welcome!

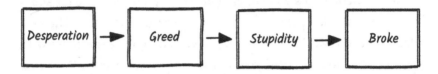

Figure 2.7: if you get desperate, you end up broke

If you don't trust me on this one, try it yourself. Get desperate to make lots of money fast thinking it will solve all your problems. See what happens. ☺ We can compare notes!

Don't get desperate, don't get greedy and there will be a higher chance of your life being free of stupidity and going broke.

Growing up on the water with boats, jet skis and scuba diving in the ocean, my uncle Jon always told me that the ocean is unpredictable — it can't be tamed or taken for granted. It is the master and you never will be. You can't control it, so don't think you can. I now have a healthy and deep reverence for the ocean, and similarly, for my investing.

I am nothing. I know nothing. I am Jon Snow.

What do the pros say?

I asked three professionals to share with me the biggest lessons they have learned when it comes to behaviour and investing. I found it interesting that there are common themes in their responses. You might too — so here is what they said.

- Kate Howitt, Institutional money and portfolio manager:

  Markets are very unpredictable, and short-term market-to-market volatility inevitably causes an emotional response. When your positions are up, it's easy to feel euphoric. When they are down, you can get despondent. Our brains evolved to survive on the savannah, not to make calm, considered investment decisions. In Thinking Fast and Slow, Daniel Kahneman differentiates between fast thinking, which is quick and automatic — and notoriously error prone — and slow thinking, which is calm and methodical. Our brains evolved to be energy efficient, so we default to fast thinking, and this is especially true when our emotions tell us there might be a tiger in the bushes. Engaging slow thinking requires us to not be overcome by emotion. So having a plan for managing your emotions is a critical part of your investment process.

  Most of the very best investors I've known don't have live prices flashing at them all day long. Nicholas Nassim Taleb, in The Black Swan, discusses how the frequency of a data series impacts whether you are looking at signal or noise. If you want signal, look less frequently — and this has the added benefit of minimising the emotional jolts you receive. You can think of market pricing like caffeine — you have to know how many 'cups' a day are best for you. For me, one coffee in the morning gets me going, maybe one after lunch, but more than that makes me too jittery to think straight. It's the same with watching stock prices. Checking in daily is helpful, but watching all day long is just going to make me high or low — neither of which will help me engage in the slow thinking that leads to good decision making.

- Jody Fitzgerald, Institutional money and portfolio manager:

The most important lesson for an investor is when to walk away. If an investment is performing poorly, it's tempting to hold onto it until we at least get back to square. We should think about the expected outcome from here. What matters is how much we expected the investment to increase from here, if at all. If the expected return is lower than other opportunities we could invest in, we should walk away. If the expected return is higher, we should be willing to hold or even increase our investment.

The same issues can occur with winning opportunities. We all have a bias towards winners. It can be hard to sell out of an investment that has performed well and appears on a never-ending upward trajectory. We need to ask ourselves the same question. How much can it reasonably make from here? For all investments, we should have a view of what we expect from the outset. Once that expectation has been met, unless something has changed or there is new information to consider, we should take our profits and move on. Recency bias and overconfidence bias can often lead to investors watching an investment hit an all-time high and then fall right back down to where it started.

Knowing when to sell is one of the most challenging investment lessons I have learned over time and one I encourage all new investors to consider. Have a plan. What would signal you to sell, and when should you buy more?

- Gemma Dale, Director of SMSF and investor behaviour, NAB:

I consider myself a pretty conservative person — I like to really understand what I'm earning and what I'm doing with my money, spend less than I earn and have a savings buffer. I always have insurance (income protection, home/car/travel etc.). Funnily enough I think that allows me to take bigger risks with investing: buying a house for the first time on a pretty modest salary as a single person, borrowing more to buy a bigger home etc. I always wanted to get rid of the debt as soon as possible so I had a flatmate, paid as much as I could into the mortgage etc.

Working in investing is quite interesting: so much information and so many opinions — not always good ones. You have to work out what kind of investor you are and what you're comfortable with. I don't always feel like I've made brilliant decisions, but if I look back, the trajectory has been incredibly positive. Some of the most confident investors I've met haven't made the best decisions — in fact their choices have been really poor. That level of confidence can be really misleading.

If there is one thing I want you to take away about developing the mindset of an investor it's that you are your life and you need to control what you can control, and let the investing happen in the background. Like me, you are nothing when it comes to investing and money. The best-performing company in the world does not care about you. It does not know you're a shareholder, and you need to know that. Focus on what you can control, and let your investing do the rest.

○ ○ ○

Next up, we're going to look at nailing your investing strategy.

The answer to the riddle at the start of the chapter is 'I am habit'.

Start with this ...

To get the most out of this chapter, consider the following money and investing questions for yourself:

* What style of budget suits your life? A bottom-up or a top-down approach?

* What sources of income are adding to your overall wealth position? Are you relying solely on investing? Consider all income streams.

* How can you level up in your career to improve your earning capabilities?

* Are you getting caught up in hype or confirmation bias when it comes to your investing? Sit back and think through investing goals that are realistic and aren't influenced negatively by others.

* Are you pacing yourself and investing with a steady, long-term wealth growth perspective, or are you looking to get rich quick?

3

Nail your strategy

The number-one mistake I see people make when investing is majoring on the minor, particularly when starting out. What I mean is, they spend too much time hung up on which broker or platform they invest with, typically looking for the cheapest fees. There's more to your investing strategy than just the broker or platform you invest through.

I have recorded close to 600 podcast episodes since starting *this is money* and I have never done an episode on 'the top investment brokers in Australia'. Why? Because it's a bit too 'click baity' for me but also because brokers and investing platforms all do the same thing. They are in the same ballpark in terms of costs and the only difference between them might be the way the app looks or functions, or some other superficial feature.

That's not to say that the broker or platform you use shouldn't make sense to you and be easy to use—that's not my point. Some brokers have asked to advertise on my podcast but I declined because they are trading heavy (their marketing efforts are to attract people who just want to buy and sell daily) but also their accounts are too confusing to use. I don't want to promote anything I wouldn't genuinely use myself or be happy for a friend or family member to use. We need to be comfortable with the platforms and brokers we use.

However, what matters more than choice of broker or platform is the ownership structure you choose, how long your money will be invested and what the tax and estate planning considerations for the investment are. You also need to understand your risk tolerance and have a solid understanding of what you're investing in. It's important to be informed when making these decisions. You need to know, for example, that a large portfolio might result in too much ongoing tax; or that you could have an adverse tax event when selling down shares if the ownership structure you've put in place is not the most appropriate one for your goals. To me, these things must come before choosing which investing platform has the prettiest app or the cheapest fees.

Too often I see comments in our *this is money* Facebook group asking questions like, 'My Spaceship portfolio has fallen 30 per cent; should I sell or hold?' That's a real-life, real-time lesson in highly concentrated tech stocks (as Spaceship invests heavily into the technology sector). If you're asking whether or not to sell because there have been price fluctuations, then you have no strategy or you weren't aware of what you were investing in — or both. Either way, it means you need to step back and design an investment strategy to help guide your decisions.

The implications of not having an investing strategy sorted might not make a huge difference if you're only investing $5 a month, but if you had a couple of hundred dollars per week you wanted to invest you'd really need to get your strategy right.

With some simple planning you can make your investing future-proof, easy and, most importantly, right for you.

I believe the five key factors that need to be considered when it comes to your strategy are (in order):

1. goals and your 'why'

2. risk profiles and time horizons

3. ownership structures for taxation and estate planning

4. selecting the right product (i.e. brokerage account or platform)

5. the underlying investment.

If you nail these five things, you will be worlds ahead of many other investors. Having covered goals and your 'why' in chapter 1, let's now talk about the other four key factors.

Technically, there is a sixth key factor to consider, which is: Do you have the money to achieve your goal and is the goal realistic? If not, you may need to reset your goal and expectations, save/earn more money or make other life/lifestyle compromises to achieve your goal. Yes, I'm in 'financial adviser' mode, but you need to know that while you may have the best strategy in place and the most awesome trust structure, you also need enough money (the actual amount will vary from person to person). If your financial arrangements are set up in a way that is too complex and expensive for your needs, you'll never achieve your goal.

Risk profiles and time horizons

As a starting point, you need to understand the concept of 'defensive assets' and 'growth assets'. The term 'asset' in the finance world refers to an investment that adds to your wealth, whether it be shares, property or even your own business. Defensive assets are typically associated with lesser risk as they perform with more certainty and predictability, and growth assets are associated with higher risk as their performance can fluctuate more but also have a greater potential for growth. Cash in a bank account, bonds and gold can be considered defensive assets, while bricks (property and infrastructure) and businesses (shares) are considered growth assets.

The higher your exposure to growth assets is, the longer you need to be invested in these if you want a higher return than you would with defensive assets (due to the possible fluctuations and volatility of growth assets). You'll pick your blend of defensive and growth assets based on your appetite for risk — whether you're a more conservative investor (preferencing defensive assets) or more aggressive investor (preferencing growth assets). This is known as your risk profile. Look at figure 3.1 to see how defensive and growth assets behave differently over a period of time. If you're a more aggressive investor you'd be ready to ride the growth wave, whether it's going up or down. It's like riding an investing rollercoaster: the highs can be amazing, but you've got to have the stomach to handle the drops and not let them phase you too much!

Another term you'll hear a lot in investing is 'portfolio', which simply means the collection of your investments. When it comes to investing through avenues such as superannuation, people mention things like '70/30' or '60/40': these reflect percentages of growth vs defensive assets that individuals have chosen to invest in. So '70/30' means 70 per cent of a portfolio is invested in growth assets and 30 per cent is invested in defensive assets. However, just check, as these abbreviations may be the other way with your selected portfolio. For example, in table 3.1 (on page 58), I start with defensive first in the table, as in 100/0 for 100% defensive.

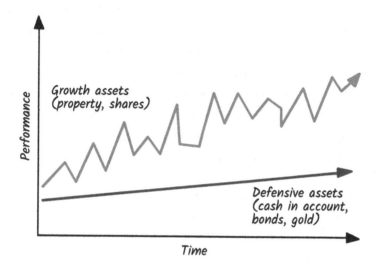

Figure 3.1: growth and defensive assets at work over time, one demonstrating more fluctuation, the other demonstrating more consistency and predictability while not necessarily seeing the same growth

You'll also often hear the phrase 'past performance is no indication of future performance' in reference to how certain portfolios have performed—though I disagree. While this is often said from a risk-mitigation standpoint, quality growth assets have always outperformed defensive assets over the long term. The more risk you're willing to handle, the greater the potential reward.

So how do you figure out your risk profile? That's a good question. In traditional financial planning, you would complete a risk profile questionnaire and it would calculate what level of risk suits your personality. Problem is, this is primarily a compliance-driven test. If you were a conservative soul who didn't inherently love taking risks, you would be placed into a more defensive portfolio, which of course means there would be less chance of your capital fluctuating and/or reducing due to market movements.

In practical terms, these traditional risk profile questionnaires fall short when, for example, a person who is aged 30 is profiled as 'conservative' invests their superannuation at 30 per cent growth and 70 per cent defensive and leaves it there for the next 30 years! This could cause financial loss to them of hundreds of thousands of dollars — they're missing out on potential growth when perhaps all they needed was a little more education. These questionnaires are useful for a financial adviser, but not everyone needs to see an adviser to start investing in shares. There are other ways you can assess your risk profile for yourself, plus, with a bit of education, you might have a slightly different risk profile than you thought.

The antidote to a younger person (or anyone, really) with a conservative risk profile is education and understanding how time horizons and growth assets work together. Back when I was a practicing advisor, I would always spend time coaching my clients around asset classes and time horizons if they are conservative investors on paper, particularly if the money doesn't need to be accessed for over 30 years. I want to stress that the main thing you need to consider when looking at your risk profile and investing is your time horizon.

Am I saying you should never invest in conservative portfolios and only in 100 per cent growth assets? No. I'm saying you need to be rock solid on your investing goals and time horizons. The fact that you're reading this book says you've either got a slightly higher risk appetite, or you want to be educated so you can feel more confident in making less-conservative investment choices. Good on you!

To understand time horizons better, you need to know which of your goals are short term, which are long term, and which ones warrant investing in shares. Financial markets work in slightly different cycles from what you might expect. A short-term financial market cycle may be three or four years! Here are the definitions I use for time horizons when I invest:

- *short term:* less than four to five years

- *long term:* more than four to five years.

There is no exact science to this, which is why I have settled on four to five years as a tipping point. However, for most pre-mixed investment portfolios that have an allocation of 60 per cent growth assets and 40 per cent defensive assets, it is recommended by investment product issuers, such as your superannuation company, to hold them for at least five years. Pre-mixed investment portfolios are ready-made portfolios with a mix of defensive and growth assets — more on this from Nick in chapter 5.

Need to save for a new car, holiday, lounge, landscaping, kitchen renovation or wedding over the next three to four years? These wants tick the short-term box and a high-interest savings account or mortgage offset account, will ensure your capital is preserved, giving you some income through interest or by not paying mortgage interest if in an offset. Why risk your capital if you need the money in the short term?

Wanting to put your kids into a private school in eight years' time and have some capital to start with? You might consider an investment account to maximise the return on your money — it will work away in the background for eight years without you having to think about it.

Pre-mixed portfolios are also a great solution if you want a set-and-forget option. Much like your superannuation portfolio, you can have pre-mixed portfolios with ordinary money (that's code for 'in your own name'). Nick will touch on portfolio construction in chapter 5.

With a bit of thought, planning and research you can determine the timeline of your goals, your risk profile and what cash you have available to invest—and off you go! But if you're the kind of person who would really benefit from having the support of a third party when considering how to set up your investing, a financial adviser could be helpful. Their job is to look at how much you will need over your time horizon and work backwards from anticipated returns from portfolio mixes. They'll make investment recommendations based on financial projections and anticipated returns. The examples in table 3.1 are of the anticipated returns that online platform Life Sherpa uses for its portfolios. You'll notice that inflation (consumer price index, or CPI) is the benchmark for all investing.

Table 3.1: anticipated returns that Life Sherpa uses for its portfolios, based on the past 20 years' performance

Portfolio	Defensive / growth split %	Portfolio target	Anticipated return based on the last 20 years
Conservative	70/30	CPI + 2%	5%
Balanced	50/50	CPI + 3%	6%
Growth	30/70	CPI + 4%	7%
High growth	10/90	CPI + 5%	8%
Global equities	0/100	CPI + 6%	9%

CPI is modelled at 3%.

These targets are handy to know when you are calculating investing amounts and what return you could expect over a period of time.

A somewhat misleading term you'll hear when referencing this blend of growth or defensive assets is 'balanced'. Most people would assume that like the balancing of scales, a 'balanced' pre-mixed portfolio would equal a 50/50 split of growth and defensive assets. Well, this is often not the case. I would caution that in the superannuation world (aka the Wild West) I have never seen a pre-mixed option called 'balanced' that has an allocation of 50/50 growth/defensive. Most balanced funds in the superannuation world are generally geared towards 70 to 90 per cent growth assets. Not much is 'balanced' about that. I would like to see some reform in this sector to make portfolio labelling uniform across the names and allocations regardless of the superannuation fund. Most ordinary people would agree that the allocations of a balanced fund should be equal.

Something that the more detailed and curious investor might be interested in when investing in the Wild West—I mean, superannuation portfolios—is that it gets murky really fast around what fund managers can call growth and defensive assets. Some superannuation funds and managers may hold unlisted (i.e. not publicly traded on the ASX) infrastructure and property assets (such as Brisbane airport or Sydney airport) with up to 50 per cent allocated to the defensive portion of their portfolios. On the other hand, a listed infrastructure asset (i.e. publicly traded on the ASX) such as Transurban (TCL) might be allocated 100 per cent growth. This is how some superannuation portfolios outperform the like-for-like portfolios of other providers. I love marketing—it's so cute—but you always have to look behind the numbers!

Unlisted infrastructure sometimes = defensive.

Listed infrastructure always = growth.

Whether you're investing in your superannuation or investing through a broker or investing platform, keep these concepts in mind. Overall, consider your risk tolerance in alignment with the time horizons for your goals. When will you be accessing your money again in future, and which of your goals could you invest for?

If you're investing through superannuation in a 'balanced' portfolio, dig a little deeper. Even a phone call to your superannuation fund can help you understand how your money is invested and why it is invested in that way.

Investing in action

Consider five short-term goals and five long-term goals. Consider the time horizons I've mentioned and which of your goals require just a high-interest savings account, and which ones could be great to invest for.

Bring up your superannuation account and check your current superannuation investment option. How much is invested in growth and how much in defensive assets? Ensure it's poised for a long-term investment strategy, particularly if you're under 50!

Ownership structures for taxation and estate planning

Ownership structure is an important aspect of investing that new investors seldom think about. By ownership structure I mean, for legal ownership and tax purposes, whose name the shares are in. If you are putting $5 per week into a micro-investing app to dip your toe into the world of investing, ownership structure probably isn't a big deal because you aren't investing huge amounts of cash. But what if you wanted to commit hundreds of dollars per week to an investing account for the long term? This needs to be planned out because once you've committed money to your investing structure it's too late to change it, and if you need to dispose of (sell) the asset, you'll be hit with the tax rates and rules of the day.

There are different ownership structure options for investing that suit different goals and time horizons. I'll detail the main ones that you may want to consider shortly.

I will not be getting into the weeds of taxation and legislation because I need you to understand the macro concepts of investing structures first. The year-on-year taxation and disposal of assets should be handled by your tax accountant because these affairs can get a bit complex and your investing blends with other income in your life. It's worth knowing that most investment platforms or brokerage accounts can be held in almost all the ownership structures shown in figure 3.2, and described overleaf, so generally you won't limit your options in that regard.

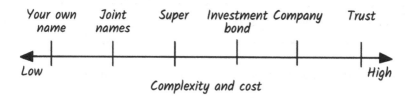

Figure 3.2: ownership structures

> Let's digress for just a moment to define a couple of investing terms.
>
> A *dividend* is a payment of profit made by the company to the owners (or you, the shareholder!). Dividends can be in the form of cash, or you can elect for the dividend to be reinvested to buy more shares automatically via the share registry. Dividends are generally paid twice per year.

(continued)

Distribution refers to the income received when you invest in ETFs or managed funds. These funds are a bundle of different shares and other assets such as bonds. The income from all these underlying assets may flow into the fund at various times throughout the year, so the fund will usually make a distribution of income received (whether interest, capital gains, or dividends) twice per year, but it could happen annually or quarterly depending on the fund. For ETFs you can also elect via the share registry to automatically reinvest the distributions into more units (or shares) of the fund.

Dividends and distributions are considered taxable income, so they become part of your personal income tax assessment each year. If you elect to automatically reinvest the dividends or distributions, they are still considered income and the automatic reinvestment is after the fact. This could mean you may need to have other money put aside for tax.

Keeping these definitions in mind, here are the options to consider when deciding on your ownership structure.

O *Investing in your own name*

You might use your own name when you're just getting started or if you need access to the investments at any time without any major issues. This is a quick and easy way to invest. It may be useful if you are single, want sole ownership of an investment or are not carrying any professional risks in your life (such as being self-employed and open to litigation). This is the least complex approach.

How tax works each year

Income from assets in your own name will be added to income earned from employment. It is taxed at your marginal tax rate (the rate corresponding to your total income) and will appear on your individual tax return. If you were on a 37 per cent tax rate, income from assets in your name would be taxed at 37 per cent (after any tax credits within dividends or distributions).

How tax works when you sell the shares

Without drowning you in tax info, let's talk about capital gains tax (CGT) briefly. 'Capital gain' refers to the profit you've made minus what you paid for an asset initially (your 'cost base'), in this case shares. When you sell your shares, you may trigger a capital gains event and be liable for capital gains tax, which is a tax on the profits you've made upon sale. It's not a one-off or separate payment; it forms part of your income tax assessment in the year you sell your shares and as such will be taxed at your marginal tax rate.

However, if you have held the asset for a period of 12 months or longer, you will be entitled to a (CGT) discount of 50 per cent. This means, if you sold a parcel of shares and you had a gain of $10000, you would only be taxed on 50 per cent of this gain, or $5000. The $5000 would go on your personal tax return as income, just like your employment income.

How estate planning is impacted

Estate planning refers to how your assets (shares, property, etc.) will be managed upon your death. Any assets that are in your own name will form part of your estate and will be distributed as part of your Will. If you haven't already, I highly encourage you to get your Will and other estate planning sorted!

The pros

This approach is simple, low cost and virtually no set-up is needed. Easy!

The cons

There's no flexibility with tax planning or asset protection (protecting your assets from potential litigation or creditors seeking repayment from you). This option might not be suitable for high-income or high-net-worth individuals who carry risk of litigation if self-employed (for example, surgeons who may be sued).

O *Investing in joint names*

This option is great if you're in a relationship and both partners are on the same income level or you wish to keep your money separate in theory but together in practice.

How tax works each year

Each partner's proportionate share (50 per cent unless otherwise stated) of income each year from the portfolio will be added to each individual's tax return and to any other employment income. In a similar way to owning the shares in your own name, if you were on a 37 per cent tax rate, income from shares in your name would be taxed at 37 per cent (after any tax credits within dividends or distributions).

How tax works when you sell the shares

Each partner's share of the assessable gain will be taxed on each individual's income tax return. Capital gains tax rules still apply and flow through as if you owned it in your own name.

How estate planning is impacted

This can be dangerous if not set up correctly or with a plan. Generally speaking, when accounts are set up in joint names, the ownership is joint or 'joint tenants'. This term comes from the property world and means if one of the parties dies, the surviving party automatically assumes control of the deceased person's share, bypassing the will/ estate of the deceased. Most share registries do not recognise the 'tenants in common' ownership structure, which relates to property and dictates that the deceased person's share of the asset goes to their estate, not to the surviving party. You need to check this if you're buying jointly held assets.

The pros

Like individual ownership, it's simple, low cost and virtually no set-up is needed. It's great for getting started and easy to split income each year or share ownership with a spouse or partner

The cons

It may be harder—but not impossible—to unwind if you wish to sever the ownership. Estate planning may be a sticking point here if there are blended families involved (multiple marriages with multiple children). There may also be issues with separation. There is no flexibility to sell assets separately. Each will realise a gain (or loss!).

O *Investing in superannuation*

This is a great vehicle for long-term, tax-effective wealth creation, plus every working adult already has a superannuation account by law. But, there are trade-offs for enjoying the favourable tax environment, namely accessibility, as you can't access your super before reaching preservation age (the age you can legally begin accessing your superannuation funds, which is between the ages of 55 and 60 in Australia depending on the year of your birth).

How tax works each year

Income from assets within superannuation are taxed internally at the superannuation rate of 15 per cent (which would generally be much lower than the marginal tax rate associated with your income outside of superannuation). Income from superannuation investments does not appear on your individual tax return because it's taxed internally within the fund. The percentage returns you see for your investment option on your statements are generally after fees and taxes. Once a member commences a superannuation pension (begins accessing their superannuation money) after age 60 and retires from the workforce, pension accounts have a tax rate of 0 per cent (up to the pension account limit).

How tax works when you sell the shares

Profit from asset sales within superannuation receive a 33.33 per cent discount for CGT. Like year-on-year income, this does not appear on your individual tax return. This is also generally factored into the unit price and return of the fund each year.

How estate planning is impacted

Superannuation is a trust, which means the assets are not held in your name — they are held 'on trust' and the superannuation company effectively acts as the trustee of your retirement savings (a trustee controls investment decisions and can change them whenever it thinks it's appropriate). Because of this, superannuation doesn't automatically go to your estate and is not distributed according to your will. The way your superannuation is managed upon your death is at the trustee's discretion, unless you make what's called a 'binding nomination of beneficiaries' nominating selected family members and qualifying beneficiaries (i.e. spouse, kids under 18 and other financial dependants). You can have your estate as a beneficiary, in which case the trustee will pay your estate. It's important to have a binding nomination of beneficiary for your superannuation as the trustee will then have to pay your superannuation balance to your beneficiaries. These documents generally require two adult witnesses and none of the beneficiaries listed can be a witness. Breathe! Still with me?

The pros

This is the most tax-effective investing you'll get! You already have an account set up and the money can grow in a relatively low-cost environment as superannuation fees are becoming very competitive within the superannuation environment. The more money you have in your super, the more money you'll have to grow tax free after age 60, if you stop work and commence a superannuation pension. Tax-free growth and income. Yes, please!

The cons

Accessibility is probably the biggest disadvantage when it comes to investing within superannuation because you can't change your mind and ask for it back once the money is committed! There could also be some legislative risks if governments of the day wish to tweak accessibility ages or internal tax rates. I believe this is a risk worth taking, as superannuation will be more favourable in terms of investing for the long term because the government will always want to incentivise people to be self-funded during retirement.

⭘ *Investing through a (discretionary / family) trust*

This ownership structure may be reserved for higher income, higher net worth individuals (or families), or those who are on track to become one. Trusts are also commonly used by those who are self-employed and operate a business as opposed to a sole trader/contractor.

A discretionary trust is generally the trust of choice for most people, most of the time, and can commonly be referred to as a family trust, as the trust deed will dictate that it can distribute income to members of the family unit.

Trusts are structures that hold assets, on trust, for the benefit of their beneficiaries. They may be used for asset protection and also for flexibility year-on-year regarding taxation.

How tax works each year

Trusts must distribute any profits to beneficiaries each year. This means that the trust will not pay tax, but the beneficiary will, at their marginal tax rate. This can be flexible with a discretionary family trust and profits distributed at the trustee's discretion each year. If there was a lower income earning spouse one year, the majority of income may be distributed to them, which in turn means paying less tax overall within the family unit.

How tax works when you sell the shares

Upon the sale of assets where there is a capital gain, the gain must be distributed to beneficiaries, much like year-on-year income. The gain would then be taxed at the beneficiaries' marginal tax rates. However, any capital losses must stay in the trust and can't be distributed to beneficiaries. Such losses can be used to offset future income in the trust.

How estate planning is impacted

Trusts do not form part of your estate nor can they be dictated in your will as the assets are not held in your name. You are a beneficiary of the trust, which is established for your benefit. If you are a director of a trustee company or individual trustee, your estate representative would step in and take control of this trust should you die. Trust deeds and company constitutions will have provisions in the event of death or changing directors/trustees.

The pros

Trusts can be seen as the most flexible form of asset ownership because each year any income and profit is distributed at the discretion of the trustee (in accordance with the trust deed). They also offer asset protection because the assets are not held in the name of any individuals. So if, for example, you were likely to be sued in your line of work, the assets held within the trust are protected.

The cons

Complexity and cost are the biggest disadvantages. You can probably tell trusts are not a simple ownership structure—costs include not only set-up costs (potentially in the thousands), but ongoing accounting and taxation costs (also in the thousands) as you're setting up an entity that will likely need its own bank account, financial reporting and tax returns each year. If you do not have enough wealth within the trust, these costs become prohibitive. This isn't an option I'd recommend to every investor. If you're unsure I'd suggest you talk to your accountant or financial adviser.

⭘ *Investing through a company*

It would be extremely rare to have your investments owned by a company, but there may be circumstances where this is the case. Examples include if a company was a beneficiary of a trust that needed to distribute income or if there were some complex asset protection strategies at play for higher net worth individuals or families. You may have heard the term 'bucket company', which is when higher net worth individuals distribute money from their trusts to companies to effectively save money on tax.

How tax works each year

The company tax rate is 30 per cent for all income and profit received by the company that is used for investment purposes only. There are no capital gains tax concessions within companies. This structure is most beneficial for high-net-worth individuals who would otherwise have to distribute funds in their own name at the highest tax rate of 47 per cent. However, by instead distributing funds to an entity with a tax rate of 30 per cent they forego any capital gains concessions.

How tax works when you sell the shares

When companies sell assets, there are no capital gains tax discounts—all profits must be taxed at the company tax rate of 30 per cent. In the event of capital losses, these can be carried forward to offset future gains within the company.

How estate planning is impacted

As companies are an entity in their own right, governed by a constitution, this document will detail what happens in the event of the death of one of the directors. If you are a shareholder and director in your own name, the shares will form part of your personal estate. If the shares are owned by a trust, they do not form part of your estate because they are an asset of the trust. Shareholding and directorship are separate.

The pros

The only real advantages are the potential tax deferral and asset protection. The reason it's a tax deferral is that while a company pays a tax rate of 30 per cent on earnings and profit, you would still need to get the money out of the company via dividends. It's an advantage because if you pay less tax now, you have more to invest and grow—you've effectively had tax money growing over the years. When you receive dividends, they are taxed at the marginal tax rate of the person receiving the dividends, with credit for tax already paid in the company.

The cons

As you are setting up a separate tax entity, there will be both initial and ongoing costs involved, such as the cost of producing company records and tax returns. As opposed to a trust, a company would be seen as inflexible for year-on-year administration, particularly if you have a family and adult children who may be studying and not working. Again, this isn't an ownership structure I'd recommend for every investor.

○ *Investing in investment bonds*

Investment bonds could be suitable for those who are on the highest marginal tax rate or those looking to have investments that can be controlled by them, including being able to elect where the investment amounts are to go should they die. These may be more useful for grandparents, uncles and aunts to set up as funds for children. They also include education bonds.

How tax works each year

Investment bonds are also known as 'insurance bonds'. While they no longer have a life insurance component, technology has allowed investment platforms to be set up within the shell of this structure. These bonds are taxed at the company tax rate of 30 per cent, though the rate is sometimes less, depending on the investments, due to the underlying tax components of dividends received. These bonds are taxed internally (paid by the bond issuer) and income does not get added to your tax return. The percentage returns you see would generally be net of taxes and fees.

How tax works when you sell the shares

Similarly to companies, there are no CGT concessions and any capital gains are taxed at the company tax rate of 30 per cent.

How estate planning is impacted

Investment bonds fall outside of your estate. You would elect a non-binding beneficiary of the funds in the event of death. This can be useful for adults who want to set up funds for grandchildren, nieces and nephews. An adult may choose to write a child as a beneficiary with a non-binding intention, for the monies to be used for the deposit of a house after age 25, for example. If circumstances change and the adult wanted to remove a child as a beneficiary, they could elect their own estate as a beneficiary, removing the child's name from the account. This could also be used as an estate-planning tool if there was a blended family or if you simply wanted to leave money to adult children. Because they are internally taxed as their own entity, changing the beneficiary is after the fact and can be left to anyone at any age.

The pros

The advantage/disadvantage pendulum swings the most with investment bonds. One advantage is that after you have held the bond for 10 years, any income drawn from an investment and received in your bank account is tax free. Another advantage is that because these bonds are taxed internally, often at less than 30 per cent for those in the highest tax bracket of 47 per cent, this means they can be seen as a 'second' superannuation or a safe haven to park wealth for estate planning. These bonds are also useful for investing for kids.

The cons

Other than the fact that there are no capital gains tax concessions within bonds, one of the main detractors is the 125 per cent rule. This rule states that each year you can only put 125 per cent of funds that you invested the previous year into the bond. So, if you made an initial investment of $10 000, you could only add $12 500 into the bond the following year. It's a use-it-or-lose-it situation. If you add more than 125 per cent, the 10-year rule is reset. This is not a deal breaker, though, because you could easily set up a second bond if you wanted to. Another disadvantage may be the cost. It's effectively an investment platform, which means there would be higher fees for investments that you may otherwise hold directly via a broker. This should not be seen as a deal breaker either, though, if you need the bond for tax or estate-planning purposes.

What structure is most appropriate for you?

You've no doubt picked up that you will see many complexities enter a chat when you pull the thread of ownership structures. This need not be the case when you put strategy first. Strategy will always come back to your 'why'. Why are you investing this pot of money in particular?

If you are clear that you want to invest for your niece or nephew, or if you want to potentially save for kids' education expenses with an investment account, you can rule out superannuation right away. When it comes to your investing and ownership structures, sometimes you need to make an on-balance call and take action. While you can't fully know or control the future, you can make an informed decision by looking at the advantages and disadvantages of an ownership structure before you invest. It's worth noting that the legislation for asset ownership rarely changes. You can also book a chat with your accountant or financial adviser to discuss your situation personally and make the right decision for your circumstances.

Here are some examples of possible ownership structures and my rationale around each. It is important to get personal advice based on your own circumstances, but this will give you an idea of how ownership structures can be used. As you read through, you'll see how varied the approaches are.

Example 1: Jesse

Current situation: Single, early 20s, living at home and starting a career.

(continued)

Goal: Wants to build long-term savings; unsure what the next five to six years may look like.

Possible ownership structure: In own name.

Rationale: This is the most flexible structure for Jesse's situation because if things change in an instant, money can be accessed and Jesse can capitalise on any CGT discounts available.

○ ○ ○

Example 2: Charlie and Taylor

Current situation: Young married couple, late 20s, own home with mortgage, both on full-time salaries.

Goal: Have an interest in investing and saving money to retire early one day; they understand longer term there may be more of a financial upside with investing as opposed to paying down the mortgage.

Possible ownership structure: In own names, equally (2 x separate accounts).

Rationale: I believe there is less flexibility with joint accounts than in own names; if one spouse stops working when starting a family, future investment allocation can be decided at the time. Not having a joint account may also assist in finding the correct risk profile or investment strategy for each individual, which is an important factor to consider when investing. Ideally, both partners should exercise caution that they are both equally engaged with their money and investments. Make sure they are educated, understand the concepts and have buy-in.

○ ○ ○

Example 3: Casey

Current situation: Single parent, 32 years old with a child who is six years old; has custody 50 per cent of the time; is working fulltime and renting.

Goal: Wants to save for a house deposit; understands this may be eight years away; is unsure if they will buy a house to live in or an investment property and continue to rent where they want to live; may also decide to continue to rent and build wealth with shares only.

Possible ownership structure: In own name.

Rationale: Flexibility. Casey is not going to consider the First Home Super Saver (FHSS) scheme as they are unsure of what the future holds at this stage but they are still interested in investing for their future. Money can be moved to super if the FHSS scheme strategy is appropriate at a later date.

○ ○ ○

Example 4: Carlos and Chenaya

Current situation: 45-year-old married couple, two early teen kids, own home with a mortgage, both working fulltime.

Goal: Want to lean into building wealth now they are both back working fulltime; no desire for an investment property.

Possible ownership structure: A blend of salary sacrifice into their superannuation and an investment account in each name (not a joint account).

(continued)

Rationale: They will not beat the advantageous tax nature of superannuation for the long term; however, as they are 45 years old, access to money is important in the event they wish to retire prior to the preservation age of 60, and access their own investments in their own name. They might invest half of the available money each month into superannuation and leave half in their own names. This should be reviewed yearly.

Example 5: Alex

Current situation: 54-year-old, adult children (19 and 21), own home with low mortgage and working fulltime.

Goal: Needs to maximise retirement savings as it has dawned on them that age 60 is knocking on the door and they have not saved as much as they thought they would have.

Possible ownership structure: 1. Superannuation: maximise salary sacrifice contributions to super up to the maximum concessional contributions. 2. Depending on disposable and spare income after maxing out super, they may open an investment account or platform and invest in their own name.

Rationale: Superannuation is accessible within 10 years for Alex. Once super is capped out, Alex may even focus on paying down the mortgage and not having an investment account in their own name. However, at this age strategy may come into play and part of that strategy is to build superannuation and then, once retired, clear the mortgage with money from superannuation (often can be cashed out tax free!). Depending on the age differences, they may look at some superannuation splitting to even out their account balances. They also listen to the podcast, *Retire Right!* Hehe.

o o o

Example 6: Jordan

Current situation: A 37-year-old single person, working fulltime, renting in the city and investing in their own name; career well established.

Goal: Would like to set up investment accounts for their two nephews, aged five and seven.

Possible ownership structure: Two investment bonds (one for each child).

Rationale: This money is in a separate investment account that accepts monthly contributions and each child is listed as a beneficiary. Jordan may decide to show the children 'their' accounts as they age and explain that birthday and Christmas money is being directed there. If in the future circumstances change and Jordan does not wish to give money to the children, the children's names can be removed and the money remains Jordan's. Another option is for Jordan to continue to build wealth in their own name and at an appropriate age or life event, sell down and make a cash gift to the children. You do not need to have a dedicated account—just build wealth!

o o o

(continued)

Example 7: Sophie

Current situation: A 48-year-old woman. Professional, working fulltime, who is a widow. One 12-year-old child. Sophie has remarried and the new partner brings two other children (aged 8 and 11) into the relationship. There was some wealth in the previous marriage but most of the money has come from life insurance proceeds.

Goal: Would like to ensure that a portion of the deceased husband's estate and life insurance proceeds is carved out and left for the benefit of her only child, away from a potential asset pool and blended family made with the new marriage.

Possible ownership structure: An investment bond.

Rationale: This money would not form part of Sophie's estate and the beneficiary would be the 12-year-old child with some intentions listed (such as that the money is to go towards a deposit for a house, education costs or travel after age 22). By specifying that the child cannot access the money before age 22—which is after 10 years—it can be withdrawn tax free. Depending on the size of the savings, there may also be a view to open a superannuation account for the 12-year-old (in their name) and seed that with some funds. This is where financial planning starts to be fun. If there were funds of up to a few hundred thousand dollars in superannuation, these could be contributed to Sophie's superannuation ('bring forward' rule, non-concessional contribution). Sophie may nominate a percentage of her superannuation to her child as a binding nomination or set up a separate superannuation account with a higher risk profile (latter option is probably preferred), with the child as a 100-per-cent binding beneficiary. This does have some restrictions in terms of access (Sophie would need to retire before withdrawing the money for the child); however, the estate planning consideration is if the shoe fits!

○ ○ ○

Example 8: Oliver

Current situation: 40-year-old, self-employed business owner. Spouse and two children. The business turns over $2.4 million per year and is stable with a focus on being more lean and efficient (less work to free up time and maintain income). The business employs eight people. The business operating entity is a company (Pty Ltd). One hundred per cent of the shares in the operating entity is owned by the couple's discretionary family trust. They own their own home with a modest mortgage. They have three investment properties and max out their superannuation contributions each year.

Goal: Wishes to diversify their investments and move away from acquiring more residential investment properties. Also wishes to consciously look at taking some money off the table and out of the business, through dividends. These dividends are paid to the holder of the shares, which is the family trust.

Possible ownership structure: Investment account owned by the discretionary family trust.

Rationale: The entity is already established with annual financial accounts so there isn't a huge additional cost. The investments would also have a layer of asset protection because the money is not in Oliver's own name. At this time Oliver is not considering a 'bucket company' as a beneficiary of the family trust to hold any investments. He will consider business cash flow and profit over the coming years.

Complexity breeds complexity

The more complex your life is, the higher the chance that you'll need more complex asset ownership structures. As you can see from example 1, where there is a young, single person just getting started and no rock-solid plans, investing in their own name works just fine. When it comes to asset protection, ownership structures and tax, you would have seen that the examples get more complex when there are blended families or business structures in the mix!

Don't fall into the trap of reading comments on online forums that say, for example, investment bonds suck, because they do have their own place in investing. Not every solution is for everyone and you should always go back to your own 'why' and your own circumstances. But remember: nuance is the first casualty on online forums when it comes to investing and personal finance — in fact, for anything!

Selecting the right product

As an investor, you need products to invest in. This is unless you go directly to the Reserve Bank of Australia and buy an Australian Government bond — but really, who does that? Actually, I had a client who did that once. That was weird. Not sure you can even do it these days.

When I say 'product', I'm talking about these main investing products:

- a brokerage account for shares and ETFs

- investment platforms and apps for investing in shares, ETFs and managed funds

- Exchange Traded Funds (ETFs) or managed funds.

These are the main products you will see and deal with out in the wild, where there are no rules. I would say superannuation and investment bonds generally fit under the 'platform' product because they also provide administrative functions and trustee responsibilities. Only the tax structure or entity holding the platform is treated differently.

You need to understand something about investment products. When you use any product, you pay a fee. Your iPhone is a product that you paid for and you use. Likewise, the ETF that you might invest in has a management fee. The more complex or premium a product is, the higher the cost. This is a universal truth. Think Toyota vs Ferrari. If you want to use something or access it, you must pay.

The good news is that compared to even just 10 to 15 years ago, with the use of technology, competition and regulation, the cost to invest has reduced dramatically.

On the regulation side, it is a common myth that financial advisers or superannuation funds receive hidden commission from various investments. For at least 10 years, no product was allowed to be issued that had hidden and/or built-in commission. However, marketers still use this as a scare tactic. They will claim that their superannuation fund or investment platform has 'no commission to advisers'. It's true: their funds do not have commission, but neither do their competitors—because no-one is allowed to.

So should you use a share brokerage account, an investment platform or an app? This is an important question, and I want you to learn the features of these main options so you can make an on-balance call in concert with the ownership structure that you'll use.

Share brokerage accounts

As part of signing up to a share brokerage account, the broker will open a cash account (bank account) in your name. You are not given any cards or documents for this cash account — it sits behind the scenes and has a BSB and account number. You transfer money to this bank account and then you may place a trade with this money. Brokerage accounts can be owned by individuals, in joint names, trusts, self-managed superannuation funds (SMSF) or companies. Your broker will directly register your holding entity with a Holder Identification Number (HIN) with the Australian Securities Exchange (ASX). This is done via the Clearing House Electronic Subregister System (CHESS), the system used by the ASX to manage share transactions and record shareholdings.

The broker's online portal will list all your holdings and you can elect to have dividends from shares or distributions from ETFs paid into the broker's cash account or into one of your other accounts, such as your mortgage offset account. The broker will charge you a fee for each trade — either a fixed dollar amount or a percentage amount — whether you are buying or selling. It's worth noting that traditional brokers like CommSec and nabTrade may have higher brokerage costs but will pass on the interest from money sitting in the cash account. However, at the time of printing, lower-cost brokers such as SelfWealth and Pearler keep any interest earned from the money sitting in the cash account. Brokers are businesses after all.

You will need to keep your own records for taxation purposes, including purchase date, amount and number of shares or units, and dividend income. When you open a brokerage account, it's a good idea to have the end in mind if you're planning to buy, hold and even trade shares over the years. You need to know the cost base for each parcel when it comes to capital gains tax. The cost base is the value of the original share purchase price (plus any brokerage). For example, if you purchased 10 shares today in CBA, that is one parcel. So make sure you have solid record keeping arrangements.

There are tools such as Sharesight (an online share portfolio tracker and reporting tool) that you can plug into your brokerage account; however, you need to make sure you have mapped your data correctly in the first instance. Solutions such as Sharesight may provide a free account for a limited number of holdings or transactions and are handy if you're using a brokerage account.

Popular brokers in Australia are:

- CommSec (and CommSec Pocket)

- NabTrade

- SelfWealth

- Pearler

- Stake.

This is not an exhaustive list.

Investment platforms / apps

Investment platforms are similar to brokerage accounts; however, they operate slightly differently. You still receive an account number and BSB to transfer your money to. Any trades or purchases will be funded from this cash account, which is on the platform. Investment platforms do not issue an individual HIN with the ASX under the CHESS system to each account holder. They operate under one centralised HIN for the platform (called an omnibus HIN).

Money invested is not held by the platform-operating company itself, but via a custodial arrangement. This means that if the operating company ceases to exist or goes under, your investment is secure because it's effectively 'on trust' for you and separate from the company.

The key advantage of investment platforms is that they automatically track all your buys, sells and dividends. They provide a one-stop shop, including annual reports and tax statements, making life so much easier. The advantage of this type of record keeping and reporting is that you can see any unrealised gains for your own tax planning.

What if you purchased an ETF weekly for five years and you wanted to know the actual tax position? It would be hard to work this out manually (although not impossible). Many investment platforms were designed for the user experience and have great apps that help you work everything out.

Some platforms (mainly app-driven ones) will not give you the choice of ownership and will be set up just in your name, which is not a bad thing if you want to get started and do not have complex affairs.

Other platforms (such as Raiz and Spaceship) may only give you access to their own in-house managed funds or other portfolios they have constructed that are their own intellectual property and are not available to the open market. So you're starting to see some of the behind the scenes complexities and differences that are apparent with investing apps and platforms. Don't stress, just learn.

Investment platforms charge fees for placing trades and generally do not pass on interest income from the cash account. They are usually cheaper on fees than share brokerage accounts because of the single HIN and the scale that can be reached with technology. These platforms can also allow fractional investing, meaning you can invest as little as $1. This use of technology has been a game changer for those just starting to invest and for lower income earners. I love that investing is accessible to anyone.

Platforms that are set up by a financial adviser for managing significant wealth may also charge a fee for the entire balance on the platform and will often pay interest on the cash account used for the platform. Again, complexity breeds complexity (and costs), and not every solution is for everyone.

Popular platforms in Australia include:

- Superhero (direct to customer)

- Vanguard Personal Investor (direct to customer)

- Sharesies (direct to customer)

- Moomoo (direct to customer)

- Colonial First State (direct and adviser)

- Netwealth (generally via adviser)

- Hub24 (generally via adviser)

- Macquarie Wrap (generally via adviser)

- BT Panorama (generally via adviser).

This is not an exhaustive list.

Finally, as with everything, there are pros and cons. There may be some limitations at the fringes when it comes to investing platforms — for example, the platform may not have access to a listed commodity product. I personally call a solution a 'platform' if it has a custodian model or single omnibus HIN. For example, Moomoo calls itself a broker, but it is not a CHESS-sponsored broker.

ETFs

Nick will thoroughly cover ETFs and index investing in the following chapters. However, the confusing thing here is that an ETF is also an investment product, like a platform or managed fund.

The reason these products are so popular is that they offer a one-stop diversified solution into a range of underlying investments, usually by way of a pre-determined index of companies. An ETF is a great one-stop shop that will allow you to focus on shovelling money into your ETFs and you won't need to focus on day-to-day individual companies.

Much like how the ownership structure forms part of your overall strategy, what you invest in will also form part of your overall investing strategy and you will likely have ETFs forming part of your core portfolio.

You may already be investing via two products: an investment platform and an ETF. Products such as ETFs have a product disclosure statement (PDS), whereas individual companies bought via a share broker do not.

CHESS-sponsored broker vs platform: the great debate

With all good marketing comes nuance and detail, and sometimes the truth is withheld or over-/under-emphasised — much like the marketers who state that 'our investments have no hidden commission'. Take one look at the law and you'll see they are stating the obvious. But it sticks and sells.

In online circles you'll likely read that individual CHESS-sponsored brokerage accounts are 'the only way to invest' because you own the shares directly. While this is true, when you look at this statement with a grain of pragmatism the argument can fall away pretty fast.

Australia is unique in having the CHESS model and even the ASX is trying to move away from it.

While I personally do not care what product you choose to invest with, I want you to be informed enough to make your own decision and, much like the asset ownership structure, you need to make an on-balance call after you have looked at the pros and cons of CHESS-sponsored brokers and platforms. Remember that *what* you buy is about one million times more important than *how* you buy it—and that's without revisiting the ownership, tax and estate planning discussion.

One of the reasons the CHESS argument can fall away pretty quickly is that the moment you hang your hat on it and you want to buy a direct share through a broker that is not listed on the ASX (say, Tesla or Microsoft), you step outside of the CHESS system. You, my friend, are now operating the way most of the world operates—under a custodian model (like the investment platforms mentioned).

Another reason the CHESS argument falls flat is because if you invest mostly in ETFs, you're buying units into a fund in which the underlying shares are held on trust for the fund. So you would only have a claim on the units in the ETF via CHESS, not the assets themselves.

A fun thought exercise for a new investor is that you likely have a superannuation balance that is significantly larger than the amount you would want to start with when investing outside super. By default, you can't get your knickers in a knot over the CHESS debate as most of your wealth is already held under custody (i.e. using the custodian model) via the superannuation trustee (as your superannuation account is a dedicated platform only for retirement savings).

My final point on the whole CHESS vs custody investing debate revolves around online discussions.

Whenever a custodian or investment platform arrangement is mentioned online by a new investor who has heard about it (and doesn't fully understand it), they get worried they will lose their money should the investment platform go under. This also goes back to clever marketing by some CHESS-sponsored brokers. The fact is, the operating company of the investment platform is separate, and the whole point of a custodian arrangement is to protect the investors' wealth and keep customers' investments under a third-party custodian arrangement. People post links to companies going under (Hallifax, BBY, Storm, etc) and to people losing their money, not realising that these posts are usually stories about high-risk brokers that offer complex investing instruments such as options, CFDs (contracts for differences) or property schemes that involve a significant amount of leverage (debt). I am yet to see an investment platform (custodian arrangement) or a superannuation fund go under and customers' money lost when they simply are allowing users to buy ETFs or shares. The platform I use does not allow options or complex trading instruments.

For most people, most of the time, the CHESS debate is actually not relevant. However, there are circumstances where, if you invested only in direct Australian shares (i.e. with no managed funds or ETFs), had significant wealth and/or had an SMSF, CHESS could be beneficial from a tax standpoint.

I felt I had to address this issue given the personal finance scene in Australia. This is because CHESS is often the lead when marketing gurus create strategies. Not long ago, a broker that wanted to promote itself as being CHESS sponsored chose not to advertise on my podcast because I told them I wouldn't lead with CHESS.

While I understand that corporate actions (like shareholders voting on topics) and dividend reinvestment schemes may be limited under a custodian arrangement, I can't see that being a deal breaker for most people.

Again, complexity breeds complexity and if you're just starting out, this is not something you need to worry about. Focus on the overall strategy, the underlying investment, spending less than you earn and investing as much as you can!

Remember: start simple, make it easy and know that when the student is ready, the teacher will appear.

For what it's worth, I personally do not hold any of my wealth directly with a CHESS-sponsored broker (I have in the past). I mainly use ETFs (I don't own the underlying funds anyway) because I value the ease of reporting and record keeping with consolidated annual reports and tax statements (so I don't have to track anything).

If you do want to hang your hat on a CHESS-sponsored broker, I still love you and am so happy you're an investor, like me.

And, by the way, if you do have a CHESS-sponsored broker and another investment app/platform, you could potentially feed all the data into the one Sharesight — or similar — account for completeness.

Investment strategies

Nick will dive deep into portfolio construction and actual investments, but as part of your strategy you need to keep in the back of your head what your style of investing looks like — and that's what I'm going to look at here.

There are only three main types of investment strategy (see figure 3.3, overleaf). It is not uncommon for people to blend these.

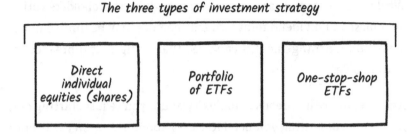

The three types of investment strategy

| Direct individual equities (shares) | Portfolio of ETFs | One-stop-shop ETFs |

Figure 3.3: the three main types of investment strategy

Let's take a look at what type of investor you'd be if you used each of these investment strategies:

- *Direct individual equities (shares)*

  You have pinpointed the direct shares that you wish to buy, you like researching shares, and you buy and hold for the long term. You understand any diversification that you are giving up and you may be a more sophisticated investor. You also enjoy trawling through company financials and all the research that comes with that.

- *Portfolio of ETFs*

  You understand that you wish to spread your risk and are not interested in trading or trying to game the system. You have an interest in investing and want to build a portfolio of different ETFs. This includes robo advisers and other offerings that have portfolios of ETFs weighted to your risk profile and time horizon.

- *One-stop-shop/diversified ETF*

  You want to keep it really simple and have one investment option in your account. The underlying investments are diversified through asset classes and countries and rebalance the portfolio automatically. Think of ETFs such as Vanguard's Diversified High Growth (VDHG) and BetaShares' Diversified All Growth (DHHF, which funnily enough uses Vanguard funds).

Getting the investment you want

It may be that you're finding it difficult to select an investment for your investing strategy because the particular product or ownership structure that most suits your needs may not have an investment that you feel comfortable investing in.

For example, I have three investment bonds: one for my niece and one for each of my nephews. While my main investment account for 'Glen's future' includes a portfolio of ETFs, the investment bond provider does not allow me to build my desired portfolio, so I have elected a one-stop-shop ETF for each bond (the Vanguard Diversified High Growth Fund (VDHG)) and for the kids' investments, this will absolutely be suitable for what I want to achieve.

If I wanted to invest in, say, the S&P 500 only for the kids and this option was not available within an investment bond, I would potentially have to have a product or ownership structure where I could house this investment because it is not 100 per cent correct for my taxation and estate-planning purposes.

Another thing to remember is that if you want to invest in, say, BlackRock's IVV, which is the top 500 US shares on any exchange and — based on your strategy — your platform or superannuation account doesn't have this exact product, it might have another fund that tracks the same index using a different fund manager. Same exposure, different fund manager.

For example, the following two ETFs track the top 200 companies on the ASX:

- IOZ: iShares Core S&P/ASX 200 (BlackRock)

- A200: BetaShares Australia 200 ETF (BetaShares).

The Vanguard Australian Shares Index ETF (VAS) tracks the top 300 Australian listed companies. (I'm not sure why Vanguard does the top 300 as opposed to the ASX 200.) However, if you wanted exposure to Australian equities and the platform or account didn't have an ASX 200 fund but it had VAS, you would choose that. The returns are almost going to be identical because companies 201 to 300 would have minor portfolio weightings. Similarly, if you wanted to use the platform 'Colonial First State, First Choice Wholesale' for whatever reason and wanted an ASX index fund, you would have to use their CFS Index Australian Share fund — which they manage — which tracks the top 300 ASX companies.

I want to drive home that even though various ETFs and different brands are popular, you can get alternative solutions that give you the same exposure as what you're after.

Once you've nailed your strategy and worked out what investment you want to make, it's time to look at the fees. At the time of printing, the fees for the two funds in my example above (IOZ and A200) — which track the top 200 companies in Australia — are 0.07 per cent and 0.05 per cent respectively. i.e. basically the same price. Because the ASX 200 is a very popular index in Australia, fund managers may or may not use IOZ and A200 as loss leaders to get customers into their ecosystem. Furthermore, due to the nature of the underlying investment, they are cheap to manage anyway.

What if your investment isn't the right one for you?

After reading this chapter you might have discovered that your ownership structure isn't ideal for your current situation. That's okay. What I would suggest is to pause and resolve what the ideal structure should be for you going forward. It's not a case of having to sell your shares today and rebuying them in another entity or account.

Instead you could do one of the following:

- *Stop salary sacrificing to superannuation* (because you have decided you may need to access these funds before the preservation age of 60)

- *Stop investing in your own name* (because you're in your 50s and you're now fairly certain that you won't want to stop working at age 60 so you're going to maximise the tax-effective nature of superannuation, both year-on-year by salary sacrificing and by growing your wealth in a tax-effective environment)

- *Not worry about your individual investment account* (because you now have a family trust set up for your business and you need to consider future wealth because your business has the chance to expose you to risk).

If you have a significant amount of money invested and you are worried about your current structure, you are likely a candidate for some personal financial and tax advice.

The point here is you can rework your strategy and leave your current investments in place and over time make a call on whether you need to sell them down and repurchase them. This would obviously trigger a tax event. Or you could leave the previous account in place and from now on put your money into a new structure. That would be okay too. You may consider it housekeeping over the next few years to clean up unused entities and accounts. There is no rush. The win here is that you have thought about your long-term strategy around your 'why' and are moving forward with that. Work closely with your accountant or financial adviser to help you decide on your next moves.

Investing is like buying a car...ish

You wouldn't wake up one day and say, 'I need to buy a blue car. I must have a blue car. Everyone has a blue car, so I must too!' and then go and buy any blue car.

You would step back and work out what type of car you need (what its purpose is; what ongoing maintenance and costs you need to consider; whether power and fuel economy are important; whether it will be hard to sell; whether it's two-door or four-door; hatch or boot). You need to work it all out.

You then decide, based on your car usage strategy, that a small hybrid SUV that seats five people and has room for a dog and a pram would be ideal. Once you've worked that out, you'd go and buy your Toyota RAV4 hybrid in blue. Now, if they don't have sky blue, only royal blue, you've made an on-balance call that it will still meet your needs. I've seen a lot of other cars in many shades of blue that are far from as good as a Toyota RAV4 hybrid!

Your future and your wealth are far more important than a car. Just as you wouldn't shop for cars solely based on colour, your investing strategy needs to be thought through on many levels. Doing things the right way will be of benefit to you, future you and the beneficiaries of your estate.

I'll now hand over to Nick for the next chapter to do all the sexy investment selection talk!

Start with this …

I've touched on a lot of deep concepts in this chapter, so let's recap. Step back and consider the following:

* Think through your risk profile in concert with the timeline of your goals. Which of your goals could benefit from investing?

* Which ownership structure feels right for your situation? Do you need to chat with your accountant or financial adviser to nut this out further?

* Which investment vehicle feels right for your situation: share brokerage accounts, investing platforms or apps?

* Are you interested in purchasing single shares, or more interested in ETFs?

* What moves do you need to make next?

4

Grasp the basics

Can you skip the rest of this book, open a brokerage account, fund it and just start buying stuff? Sure. Would that be unwise? Probably. If you've read this far into the book, you might as well keep going and learn a few basics to make you a better overall share investor.

Why invest at all?

Glen has already walked you through your personal 'why' for investing, but why do investors choose to invest in shares? What do they offer?

At the fundamental level, people become investors and buy shares because they want a financial instrument that has a historical track record of outpacing inflation and the available 'risk-free' interest rate (which government bonds don't offer). Risk-free is in quotes because nothing is truly risk free — you are always risking something — but the standard risk-free rate can be boiled down and is generally accepted as United States Treasury Bonds. Since these bonds are backed by the full faith of the US federal government they are the global benchmark for what is considered to be a risk-free rate. This impacts investors all over the world as many countries invest in US treasuries because of the perceived stability. So it is not just a US investment, but a global one. China, for instance, is the largest holder of US treasuries in the world.

The US Treasury's aim with its bonds is not to beat inflation, so if you choose this 'risk-free' money you risk losing out to the inflation rate, which is historically around 3 per cent per year. This all means that you need to find an investment that is growing faster than that historical inflation rate.

Beating inflation is your primary case for investing, but that doesn't answer the question of why you should buy a specific share, ETF or fund. At a more personal level, most people invest to secure a financial nest egg so they can either retire or, at the very least, live life on their own terms (LOOT) — that is, be able to do side gigs, work part-time or not work at all.

Before we get into any of the basics of investing, sectors, economic cycles and all the starting points for investing, let's look at why you need to start investing early and often.

The magic of compound investing

Albert Einstein called compound interest the eighth wonder of the world saying, 'He who understands it, earns it; he who doesn't, pays it'.

While some people question whether the quote was in fact from Einstein, the power of compound interest is unquestionable. And if the man who came up with $E=Mc^2$ is impressed by compounding interest, I think we should be too.

Let me pose to you a scenario, dear reader:

In 30 days you can have one of the two options below. Which do you choose?

1. A lump sum of $1 million after 30 days or ...

2. A magical penny given to you now; its amount will double every day for the coming 30 days—that is, it will become $0.02 tomorrow, $0.04 the day after tomorrow, $0.08 two days after tomorrow, and so on ...

Which did you choose? One million dollars is a lot of coin and many people would go for the $1 million after 30 days option, but that would be the wrong choice if you were trying to maximise your return. Because after 30 days that magical daily compounding/ doubling penny would have become $10.7 million dollars!

This is the power of compounding returns: your principal would accumulate with interest reinvested during the investment period, yielding more returns. The longer the investment period, the more you will benefit from compounding (see figure 4.1, overleaf).

The deal with compounding, however, is that it takes time— more than 30 days ☺. So the earlier you get your investments compounding, the better it will be for you in the long run. Let's look at another example to see what Einstein was talking about.

Craig is a bricklayer. Bricklaying is hard work. Craig saw how hard bricklaying was on his dad once he got into his 50s and decided he didn't want the aches and pains that his father has. So he started investing in low-cost index funds very early in his career. When he started investing, the balance of his account was mainly from his $500-a-month contributions.

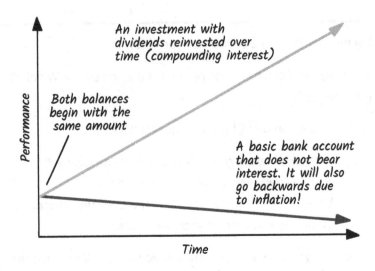

Figure 4.1: the long-term power of compounding returns

After 10 years, his total contributions had amounted to $60 000 but his portfolio was worth over $135 000 — more than twice as much as he had contributed! At this point Craig was able to see the compounding really kick in! Another 30 years passed — it was now 40 years since his first investment contribution as an 18-year-old bricklayer. His total account was now worth 13 times his contributions.

After 40 years he had invested $240 000, but his retirement account was worth over $3 184 000 (assumed approximate return of 6.5 per cent and inflation of 3 per cent, not including fees or taxes).

Do you want to retire with a $1 million portfolio?

Time is *on* your side when you are young and *against* you as you get older. Here's how to invest if you want to retire at 60 with a $1 million portfolio.

Let's assume you want to retire at 60 with a 10-per-cent annual return.

- From the age of 20, you should invest $178 a month.
- From the age of 30, you should invest $477 a month.
- From the age of 40, you should invest $1370 a month.
- From the age of 50, you should invest $4900 a month.

The power of compound investing should motivate you to get started as soon as possible. Looking at these numbers strikes fear in me to get a time machine, go back to 2001 and buy as many Amazon shares as humanly possible. But since I can't figure out the quantum realm like they did on *Ant-Man*, I think the next best thing is to have a broad understanding of share markets and make wise investment decisions with the time I have left.

For those of you who are not quite ready to invest — perhaps, as Glen mentioned, you might be retraining, down to one income with a young family, or studying to join the workforce for the first time — stay focused on building the best income you can. But once you have your hands on that sweet, sweet income, I encourage you to invest as soon as you can.

Who should you listen to?

With the rise in popularity of YouTube share pickers in recent times, retail investors have been ignoring the fundamentals of investing and blindly following a random stranger with a slick YouTube video. That 'strategy' — for lack of a better word — might have worked in a raging bull market like the one we experienced from 2012 to 2021. But just because an investment went up doesn't mean it was a wise choice. It could just have meant you got lucky for a while, and for most people that luck runs out at the start of the next market cycle: the bear market (see figure 4.2). A good example is the cult following of Cathie Wood combined with YouTube share pickers and retail investors.

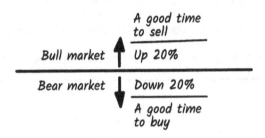

Figure 4.2: the definitions of 'bear market' and 'bull market'

Cathie Wood, manager of the technology-driven ARKK fund, was unbeatable from 2018 to 2020. Magazines were hailing her as the next Peter Lynch and comparing Warren Buffett's dusty and 'out-of-touch' investing style to Wood's hyper-tech, super growth style.

So, to no-one's surprise, if you wanted to get people to watch your YouTube video, you just talked about Cathie Wood and told your followers to buy the same shares she did. And during the bull market that worked: from 2014 to 2021 Wood's flagship ETF ARKK fund had a total return of over 600 per cent, going from $22 per share to a high of $152. But as tech shares lost favour in 2022 and earnings per share multiples began to come down to fair market values, the shares that gave ARKK such impressive numbers began to pull performance down very fast.

As of December 2023, the AARK fund had not only given back every penny it made over the previous four years, but was trading at around $50 per share, down more than $100 from its peak. And that was after a 70 per cent return in 2023! This is not to say that

Cathie Wood is a bad money manager. She has a very specific niche in hyper-growth tech disruptors that may do well in the future, but has proven to be shaky in interest-rising environments such as the one we had in 2022.

Every investor who either bought into the ARKK fund when it was on its great run or who tried to copy Cathie Wood's risky investments found themselves under water — and most likely under water a *lot* in 2022 or maybe beyond. They were looking at –50 per cent to –90 per cent returns in some cases and asking themselves, 'Why did I buy this share?' If the only answer they could come up with was 'because someone told me to', that was *not* a good answer.

So what should you consider when you're looking to buy a specific individual share of stock? Well, it is important not to rely on luck. Sure, luck helps, but there are many factors at play when you decide to become an investor in individual shares. I think to be smart you should have a cursory understanding of the following basics of share investing.

The six basic types of shares

Let's have a look at the six basic types of shares of publicly traded companies that are available for you to invest in.

1. Growth shares

These shares are from companies that reinvest all of their earnings into themselves to facilitate exponential growth. They likely won't pay a dividend (or may pay a very small one) and are often found in the technology sector. Examples include Nvidia, Uber and Altium (ASX:ALU).

Some growth companies, especially new ones, won't create profit for three to five years or maybe longer. So the growth of the company and of the share price depends mainly on speculation about what the future company is going to be worth. They have a proven concept that seems to indicate it could grow into a large company, but many times, on paper, these companies are not generating a profit.

Uber, the ride-sharing hyper-growth company, is a good example. Although it has been in business since 2011 and has been a publicly traded company since 2019 known virtually everywhere around the world, it has been unable to turn a profit on a net basis. In 2022, Uber reported a profit on an adjusted EBITDA basis, meaning it had generated positive earnings before interest, taxes, depreciation and so on. However, the company still lost a large sum of real, countable money. Charlie Munger—who, before his passing, was vice chairman at Berkshire Hathaway—famously said that 'every time you [see] the word EBITDA, you should substitute the word "bullshit" earnings'.

Uber finally hit profit for the first time in its company's history in 2023.

2. Cyclical shares

Cyclical shares are from companies that move with the economic/ business cycle. (I will talk more about the economic cycle shortly.)

Cyclical companies usually sell products and services that consumers tend to buy more of when the economy is doing well and less of when the economy is doing poorly.

Examples include cruise lines, airlines and recreational suppliers.

In 2020, when no-one in the world was flying or going on cruises, these shares plummeted. Yet in the 2nd quarter earnings of 2023, companies such as American Airlines and Delta Airlines reported record earnings. And when the world was at a standstill, companies like ARB made a killing with their recreational vehicle sales—but that was most likely a blip in the system rather than a sustainable sales boost.

3. Blue chip shares

These shares are from companies with excellent reputations and brand awareness that have been around a long time, have stable earnings and typically pay a dividend. These are sought after by dividend investors for quarterly or monthly income. Examples include Coca-Cola, Procter & Gamble, BHP Group and Commonwealth Bank of Australia.

Famously, Warren Buffet has been a long-time shareholder of Coca-Cola and has bragged about Coke's stability, brand recognition and maybe most importantly its slight growth while paying an attractive dividend.

4. Speculative shares

These shares are from companies with massive potential upsides but just-as-large potential downsides. They are extremely volatile and will add extra risk to your portfolio. If you can handle the risk, consider them. If risk is a scary word to you, stay away.

Examples are EV start-ups — some of which haven't yet produced a single vehicle — and micro-sized pharmaceutical companies that are working on a breakthrough drug but still have years of governmental testing and approvals to go before they have a marketable drug for the average person to use. When you buy into one of these companies you need to be willing to see all your money go to zero, because one government rejection for a new pill or medicine, or a bad quarter, and these companies could run out of money and be bankrupt in days.

5. Defensive shares

These shares are from companies that provide stable and consistent earnings no matter what the overall market is doing. These companies sell products and services that people need 365 days a year, regardless of income level or the economy. Examples include McDonald's, Woolworths, Verizon and Walmart.

Recession or no recession, people are *not* going to stop getting their McDonald's. Life is too hard to not have those French fries in your life. You might drop your Starbucks intake a little bit during a recession but you will probably still eat at McDonald's.

6. Dividend shares

Dividend shares are from companies that pay out a portion of their earning to investors so that you, as an investor, can start building cash flow from holding your shares. Examples include AT&T, Realty Income, SmartCentres and Charter Hall CHC.

Investors buy shares from these companies many times over in the hope of reinvesting their dividends to buy more shares and create a snowball effect for their portfolios. Or they buy shares from these companies hoping for a little bit of upside growth (to beat inflation) while taking a 3 to 5 per cent dividend each quarter or month to help pay the bills in retirement.

Economic cycles: what to invest in and when

Now that you've evaluated the six major types of shares, I really want to get into diversification, but I think it will be helpful if we touch on the economic cycle — also called the business or market cycle — first. When you have at least a basic understanding of this cycle you can have a general expectation of what the future may hold and it might give you a better idea of when to buy what type of shares.

For example, you want to buy shares in Google but you don't know if now is a good time for growth shares. Or you like the case for a bond ETF, but is now a good time to add bonds to your mix? If you are trying to get a base case for this purchase, you can take a quick look at the economic cycle to see if now is a good buying time.

The economic cycle describes and visualises the process of the economy going through the four major cyclical phases: expansion, peak, contraction and trough. In layman's terms, that's fancy talk for trying to predict if you are coming out of a recession or heading towards a recession. Although it may not feel like it, the economy is always in between recessions, so you may want to know how close we might be to the next one, and the cycle helps identify that for you — or at least helps give you an idea. But it is not a crystal ball.

The economic cycle is one of the most influential forces in the share market. It is significant because it plays a large role in determining corporate profits, which is probably the most important factor that influences share prices.

Share-market sectors are sensitive to different stages of the economic cycle. Said simply, some sectors may outperform when the economy is growing, while others may outperform when the economy is declining or in a recession.

Many professional investors make a living by rotating in and out of the various asset classes shown in figure 4.3 (overleaf) as they anticipate a change in the cycle. You may not want to be that hands on with your investments, but let me hit on the main points briefly because this is something I wish I had been taught 20 years ago when I started investing.

Figure 4.3 illustrates an example of how asset classes typically perform throughout the economic cycle. Again, this tool gives you a high level—also known as macro level—look at the economy. If your uncle is telling you at the BBQ that a recession is right around the corner you could pull up this chart and you can quickly agree or call bull crap.

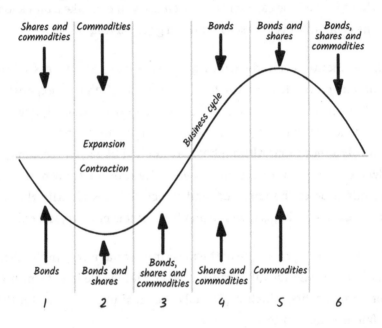

Figure 4.3: the six stages of the economic cycle, and how certain sectors behave throughout these stages

In order to see where we are in the economic cycle it helps to pull up the current performance of the major three types of assets that are traded in markets all around the world: shares (equities), commodities (i.e. anything like produce, oil, precious metals, agriculture, gold and silver) and bonds (fixed income).

Stage 1

When the economy is entering into a recession or might be in a recession and has fallen from expansion (growth) into contraction territory you might be able to identify this if you look up the performance of those three asset classes. As figure 4.3 indicates, if bonds are doing well, and shares and commodities are doing poorly, this is a sign we are heading towards a recession. This happens because bond prices rise as interest rates decline. Therefore, economic weakness favours a loose monetary policy and the lowering of interest rates, which is bullish for bond holders.

Stage 2

Here we see the bottom of the trough and the lowest point in the contraction phase of the cycle. This typically also aligns with the bottoming of the share market's decline. Even though economic conditions have slowed or stopped deteriorating, the economy is still not in the expansion phase and might not actually be growing in terms of gross domestic product (GDP). But the share market is forward looking and might anticipate the expansion phase by bottoming before the economy actually does. In stage 2 shares join bonds in the positive performance while commodities are still negative.

Stage 3

As the economic recovery gathers momentum, shares, bonds and now commodities join the positive performance party. This starts with a preparation into the expansion (growth phase) of the economic cycle. Typically, at this point the news might start asking things such as, 'Is this the bottom or a false bull trap for the shares market?'

Stage 4

My favourite stage of them all, at least in the beginning, because I don't hold very many bonds. ☺ This marks a period of full expansion. Stocks and commodities are in full-steam-ahead mode but bonds begin to turn lower because when the share market and economy are booming, fears of inflation start to rise as well putting pressure on the bond markets. To fight inflation, federal banks begin to raise interest rates.

Stage 5

The peak. I've been through a few unforgettable peaks: 2001, 2008, 2018, 2021. Hmm, maybe there is a pattern with 1s and 8s? Anyway, not all peaks are created equal. Some peaks are a bubble. Some are a 'black swan event' (black swan is an event rarely seen yet has disastrous effects. This was made popular in a book of the same name by investor Nassim Nicholas Talib). And some peaks are just normal expansion into contraction, kinda like a needed nap for the economy.

In stage 5 we are officially in an expansion phase, albeit at the end of it. The economy will be growing at a slower rate, and interest rates will be rising. Shares anticipate this decline by peaking before the expansion in the economy actually ends (remember: shares are forward thinking). In stage 5, commodities will be good performers, while shares and bonds will not be.

Stage 6

The last phase before starting over again, stage 6 marks the deterioration in the overall economy as the business cycle prepares to move from an expansion phase to a contraction phase. Shares have already been moving lower during this time, bonds have been low for two phases and now commodities join the poor performance in anticipation of decreased demand from the economy slowing. Sometimes we forget that the economy runs on all sorts of commodities: from copper and lumber to build houses, to gold and silver for telecom networks, and even cattle and pork products for food. When the economy slows, the prices of these commodities fall.

Then it starts all over again.

So, do you need to be a business cycle specialist to make money and invest in the share market? No. But could it help stop you from jumping into the next hot thing just when that hot thing is about to fall out of favour? I think it could.

Investing in action

Before we go rushing into portfolio construction, let's reinforce what we've learned.

We've just gone over the market and business cycles. Do a quick internet search and look up the YTD prices of stocks, commodities and bonds. Then use that information to try and formulate a guess for where you think we are at the moment.

Diversification

You now need to decide how you're going to diversify your portfolio. Like a great meal, a great share portfolio should have many different offerings. You don't just eat a steak and call it a day, do you? No, you need salad, rice, potatoes and maybe a side of mixed veg. And no meal is diversified without dessert!

The point of diversifying your portfolio is to help reduce your risk across various types of asset classes, sectors and sometimes varying financial instruments. This is where your risk profile, developed with Glen's guidance, comes into battle. Our goal is to try and find a balance between what you're comfortable investing in and what will perform.

Some people think of diversification first and foremost by having a portfolio of shares and bonds. Bonds are a way to make money from a company or county with a lower risk than with shares. With bonds you loan your money to an institution for a promise of a monthly or quarterly payment to you and the full return of your money at some future date. Bonds do not give you growth in the company — only the agreed-upon interest payment. And while, yes, bonds are a popular way to diversify because you're using various financial instruments, you can also have a 100 per cent portfolio of shares and still be diversified.

Let's look at Courtney's investing journey as an example.

Courtney has worked at the American department store Macy's for 10 years. She started in college and continued working part-time after she had kids. Even though she was only ever a part-time worker, Courtney was eligible for the Macy's Employee Share Purchase Plan. So from her very first payday Courtney would put aside money to purchase Macy's shares and Macy's would match them with 15 per cent.

By purchasing $100 worth of shares per fortnightly pay via an automatic purchase plan, Courtney was able to amass around $35 000 in Macy's shares over 10 years.

This was a great financial decision and really worked out well for Courtney. But with the rise of Amazon and the fall from grace of most department stores, Courtney realised maybe she should do something with this single share investment portfolio.

So, after meeting with a financial adviser, she sold 80 per cent of her Macy's shares and diversified into other types of shares. She was still young and looking for aggressive long-term growth, so her diversification plan was to go from 100 per cent consumer discretionary shares (Macy's) into consumer discretionary utilities (Chevron), technology (Apple and Tesla) and some defensive shares (McDonald's). Now her portfolio has various share sectors to provide her with diversification, but it is still 100 per cent shares (equities).

Diversifying across sectors and industries

In the case study above, Courtney was only invested in one share and one industry. She did herself a huge service by diversifying out of that one share and spreading her risk across different sectors. Courtney chose not only to diversify in different shares, she also avoided the risk of one single sector falling by diversifying across multiple sectors. If department stores have a bad quarter, or year, it's likely that her utility Chevron shares may do well to help offset her under-performance in Macy's shares. Likewise, if Chevron has a downturn from a global fuel surplus it's possible that Apple or Tesla could do well. And if all else fails, even in a recession it has proven true that people will still go out and eat at McDonald's. By diversifying across different sectors, Courtney has developed a safer portfolio while still being 100 per cent in shares. But what if she wanted to invest in something besides shares?

Diversifying across asset classes

Up to this point we've only looked at diversifying in shares. However, if you want to lower your risk more than just across share sectors you could look into diversifying across asset classes.

Asset classes refers to categories of financial instruments with similar characteristics and behaviour in the market. For example Microsoft, Coke and Woolworths are all very different companies but they are in the same asset class called equities or shares. The three traditional asset classes are shares (equities), bonds (fixed income) and cash equivalents (money market instruments). As we saw earlier, bonds give you a fixed rate and you usually get your money back after a fixed time. Unlike with shares, you don't own any of the company with bonds — you are just lending the company your money. A money market is when a bank or brokerage firm takes your money and gives you a place to keep it while you search for your next investment. It's similar to a savings account.

Additionally, alternative investments such as real estate, commodities and cryptocurrencies are often considered as separate asset classes. Each asset class has its own risk and return profile, making them suitable for different investment goals and risk tolerances.

Understanding asset classes is crucial for investors as it provides a framework for constructing a diversified investment portfolio. Each asset class responds differently to economic and market conditions, so a diversified portfolio is less susceptible to the impact of a downturn in any single sector. For instance, when shares perform poorly, bonds or other assets may provide stability or even positive returns, balancing the overall performance of the portfolio — but not always.

For instance, in 2022 we saw central banks across the globe begin to raise interest rates. When banks raise rates, it has a negative effect on the price of current bonds. If someone was trying to be safe in 2022 by having 100 per cent of their portfolio in bond funds as a 'safe haven', they would be realising the importance of diversification even in something like bonds. In 2022, the iShares 20-year Treasury Bond ETF (TLT), widely known as a 'safe' investment, finished the year with a negative performance of 31.24 per cent!

This is where looking into non-correlating asset classes can help take you from diversified to super diversified by investing in asset classes outside the top three, including areas such as real estate, commodities and cryptocurrencies.

These don't have to be big and scary. The largest investment many people have is their own home. It is arguable whether that should be considered an investment or not, so if you don't want to include your own home as an investment, or you don't own a home and want to get into real estate, you can purchase a REIT (Real Estate Investment Trust). A REIT gives you ownership in a company that owns real estate. Therefore, as real estate appreciates and collects rent you typically get a dividend payout — like a quarterly rental income. You can invest in many types of REIT: commercial property, residential rental property, industrial and so on. More on REITs shortly.

Commodities can be invested in many different ways as well. The easiest and quickest for most investors would be to buy them in the form of an ETF. You can select broad market ETFs such as the Global X Physical Precious Metals basket trust or the Betashares Crude Oil Basket ETF; or for food commodities look for something like Betashares Agriculture ETF.

Finally, let's touch on the newest asset class of the bunch, cryptocurrency. I personally own cryptocurrency and I do see the case for it as a hedge for my portfolio. As cryptocurrency is not connected to the stock market it should theoretically work as a hedge for your shares investments. I did the maths and, as of the time of writing, crypto — specifically Bitcoin, but a few others as well — is just under 1 per cent of my net worth. In keeping with the idea of diversification, these asset classes could form a small part of your portfolio as a hedge, not as a get-rich-quick scheme.

REITs (real estate investment trusts)

Have you always wanted the financial benefits of being a landlord but only have $1000 in your pocket? Then REITs may be for you! Investing in REITs can be a valuable addition to your investment portfolio, providing exposure to the real estate market while offering more liquidity than actually buying a physical property.

What are REITs?

REITs are companies that own, operate or finance income-producing real estate in various sectors, such as residential, commercial, industrial or healthcare. They are structured in a way that allows them to pass most of their income to shareholders in the form of dividends. The dividend from a REIT is traditionally higher than a dividend share as they are designed to be paying out more of their revenue than the average dividend share. REITs are known for their dividend income. They generally distribute the lions share of their rental income to shareholders. Make sure you understand the expected dividend yield and whether it aligns with your income objectives.

Types of REITs

There are different types of REITs, including equity REITs (which own and manage income-producing properties), mortgage REITs (which invest in mortgage loans or mortgage-backed securities) and hybrid REITs (which are a combination of equity and mortgage REITs). Then there are REITs in various sectors. You could own an equity REIT that specialises in commercial property, office property, shopping centres, retail homes or strip malls. Keeping an eye on larger macro trends can help you identify which type of REIT you'd like to own. For instance, if industrial warehouse space is in high demand you might want to check out REITs that lease industrial warehouses. But as places like the shopping centre are continuing to fall out of favour, maybe don't put all your REIT allocation into a REIT specialising in shopping centres.

Risk factors and liquidity

Like any investment, REITs carry risks. These risks may include market risk (real estate market fluctuations), interest rate risk (particularly for mortgage REITs) and credit risk (for mortgage-backed securities). Be aware of the specific risks associated with the REIT you're considering. REITs are typically traded on major share exchanges, which provide liquidity. However, the share price can be subject to market volatility, so consider your investment horizon and risk tolerance.

Examples of REITs

Just as with any investment, diversification is essential. It's probably best not to put all your money into a single REIT. Consider spreading your investment across multiple REITs or asset classes instead.

Some of the larger REITs in Australia include:

- Charter Hall Group (CHC)

- GPT Group (GPT)

- Dexus (DXS)

- Goodman Group (GMG)

- Scentre Group (SCG).

If you have a particular interest in diversifying into listed property, you may feel you wish to spread your risk and follow an index approach. Enter the diversified Vanguard Australian Property Securities Index ETF (VAP). This fund has weighted exposure to 33 REITs that cover residential, office, retail and industrial assets. A really interesting exercise is to look up some of the individual

REITs listed to see some of their holdings as they would be places you've been or seen. Then, look at the 33 companies in the VAP ETF and you will see more popular names, such as Stockland (is that your small, local shopping centre?).

Diversifying beyond your border

Another popular diversification strategy is to look beyond the equities in your own country and diversify into other countries. Most recent estimates say that the United States holds around 29 per cent of the world's wealth. A fund invested in the S&P 500—the 500 largest companies in the United States—helps diversify your portfolio across 500 companies represented in 29 per cent of the world's wealth. But that means if you only invest in the S&P 500 fund you're missing out on the other 71 per cent of worldwide wealth creation and returns for your portfolio. If you're interested, Australia came in at 2 per cent of the world's wealth. So to properly diversify your investment portfolios it might be prudent to add in some international investments as well.

The easiest way to gain international exposure to your portfolio is through a diversified ETF. We will address more specific ideas for portfolio construction in chapter 6, but you could look into funds such as Vanguard's VGS, which invests in 1500 companies in 23 different countries excluding Australia. Or, similarly, iShares Global 100 ETF IOO.

○ ○ ○

So, diversification is important. But how many shares is enough?

Is there such a thing as too many shares in your portfolio? For the average investor not trying to start their own hedge fund, probably not. The S&P 500 index, as you probably know, is made up of 500 companies. The ASX 200, as its name suggests, has 200. Berkshire

Hathaway, on the other hand, holds 53 companies in its portfolio. The problem for most individuals is that having 15 to 20 shares in your individual portfolio might be most people's maxing point due to the research needed to make individual investments and properly manage them (including record keeping).

Chapter 6 is dedicated to individual share ownership. But just quickly, I'd like to mention that if you are trying to own, let's say, 20 blue chip shares—10 from the ASX 200 and 10 from the S&P 500 index—and you are going to do it properly, there needs to be a *lot* of research before hitting the buy button on your brokerage account.

Even a quick scan to narrow down 700 companies to 20 companies would take a lot of time. Then the upkeep and mental toll it takes to keep your eye on your individual shares is another job. So ask yourself, 'Self, do I want to spend my free time reading company financial statements, daily news and annual reports, and making quarterly conference calls? Or do I want to be diversified in my investments and then go surfing or lay on the beach?'

If you chose the beach, you're probably better off going with an ETF. If you chose to be a financial investigator of companies, you might be ready to choose individual shares. This is another example of using the power of index funds in your portfolio.

Let's revisit the $250-per-month, dollar-cost averaging strategy. Back in chapter 2, when Glen was working out a budget and setting your behaviours before investing, he gave an example of investing 1 per cent to get started in investing while you sort out your budget, savings and debt payoff. So let's use that example of how with as little as 1 per cent you can invest and be diversified at the same time.

If you make $70000 a year and invest 1 per cent to get started you could be investing $700 a year at about $58 a month. That $58 a month invested in any of the three different index ETFs below would enable you to maximise your diversification with the simplicity of just three purchases:

- iShares S&P 500 ETF (IVV) — holds 500 companies

- Vanguard Australian Shares Index (VAS) — holds 302 companies

- Vanguard MSCI Index (VGS) — holds 1546 companies.

So instead of owning 20 shares of one company or half a share of another company you'd be owning partial shares of hundreds of companies. The same monthly amount with much more diversification and less time focused on managing and building your portfolio.

Dollar-cost averaging vs lump-sum investing

Before we bid farewell to this chapter, I want to touch on the idea of dollar-cost averaging (DCA) vs lump-sum investing. DCA is when you invest smaller amounts regularly, say, on a fortnightly or monthly basis. Glen gave a practical example of this earlier and I want to reiterate this method. Lump-sum investing is the approach where you invest a big amount of money at once, perhaps building up funds to invest on the side each time you're paid.

An example I give on the *this is investing* podcast is your grandma (hey granny) giving you a financial gift of $10 000 when you finish university. Now, you could choose to invest this as a lump sum (timing the market) or take the DCA approach and invest $500 a month until that full amount is invested (taking a total of 20 months). Which approach wins?

There have been various studies done on which is the better way to do this. Each study considers various factors that can sway the results, making them unique. Kinda like you! You know you best. Are you the type of investor who wants to set alerts for specific prices, to wait months — maybe years — on end getting fed up watching your friends make money while you wait for the next market dip? If that doesn't sound like you, you should probably join the millions of people around the world who DCA their way into wealth over the long term.

If you are that patient investor who can wait years while stacking cash for the next crash, then you should probably write an investing book — and send me a copy. ☺

Talk to Glen and he'll always say the best thing you can do for your investing is to keep investing regularly. That's why he encouraged you to have your finances sorted — because you want to be able to start investing and keep investing. Don't interrupt your investing flow! DCA is hands free, you can set and forget and let your money grow without fretting on whether this is best share price you're going to get.

o o o

Look at me rushing into things! In this chapter we've covered the basics of investing at a higher level. In the next chapter we're going to dig a bit deeper into portfolio construction, starting with index investing. See you there.

Start with this ...

There's plenty to think about after reading this chapter. I want you to spend some time pondering the following:

* Are you keeping in mind that investing enables you to make the most of your money by beating inflation and letting compounding work its magic?

* Can you remember the six, or at least two, basic types of shares?

* Could you explain the economic cycle to someone else? Flick back for a refresher.

* How are you going to diversify your investments? Look at ways to spread your investing across sectors or industries, mixing up the asset classes or investing in companies overseas.

5

Build your portfolio: index investing

(Nick)

The easiest way to get rich is to invest and forget. As John Bogle, the godfather of index funds and founder of Vanguard Funds, said, 'Buy right and hold tight'. Back in Bogle's day you had much fewer choices when you went to start investing. As recently as the 1990s, people were still calling their brokers on a telephone connected to the wall to place a share trade. (Perhaps this is a wiser way to invest, as you are less prone to log on to your broker via your phone and make a buy or sale for every little move in the market?) And although the first mutual (or managed) fund was created in 1890, 100 years later many, if not most, people were still primarily listening to their broker's advice for share picks and portfolio creation.

If you've seen the movie *The Wolf of Wall Street* you've gained a glimpse into what the life of some Wall Street stock brokers was like in the 1980s and 1990s. There is a scene where Mark Hanna, played by Matthew McConaughey, takes his apprentice Jordan Belford, played by Leonardo DiCaprio, out to lunch on the top floor of the firm's Manhattan high rise. As they eat their lobster and drink cocktails, McConaughey tells DiCaprio what the business is all about. According to the movie it is not about doing your best for the client — it is about collecting the commission! Once you've collected that commission, start planning on how you will obtain the next commission. It doesn't matter if the client makes or loses money, as long as the broker makes their commission.

So if that truly was the attitude back then, it is no wonder that our parents, who were investing in that era, may not have taught us the best way to choose shares. They probably never learned themselves, and the people they paid to invest for them were possibly only ever in it for themselves.

How to pick your investments

So where do we go from here? We know we need to invest and we have the head knowledge that investing is the best way for us to generate wealth, but *how do we actually pick* what to invest in? That's what I'll be covering in this chapter. Together, we will explore:

- index funds (including core and satellite investing)

- building your portfolio for growth (including the three-fund portfolio)

- life stage / target date fund investing.

Think of it as baking a cake or building with LEGO except your entire future depends on your ingredients. No pressure, right?

Side note: if you are reading this and have competed on the *LEGO Masters* show, that's brilliant! Shoot me an email. I'd love to have you on the podcast.

Let's address some fears about that cake metaphor. Over time, I have identified three major fears that people describe when trying to make an investment, especially if they are new to investing:

1. *Fear of picking a bad investment*

    A major fear point many people have with investing is the pressure to pick correctly. Different types of fears are associated with that pick. A top fear is choosing an investment, making a purchase and then, as soon as they do, the price drops and so does some of their initial capital — leaving them to wonder if they chose correctly, and reinforcing their fears that investing isn't for the average person.

2. *FOMO — Fear-of-Missing-Out on a good investment*

    You make an investment choice and things are going okay: you're averaging 7 per cent per year with not too much volatility. *However*, your neighbour got a hot share pick. They purchased shares in the hottest electric-vehicle (EV) start-up and his price has gone up 5000 per cent. Now your perfectly good 7 per cent seems like small potatoes and you, red with envy, begin searching for the next hot share, leaving your investing process in the dust.

3. *Being overwhelmed with choice*

    With literally the *world's* publicly traded companies at your fingertips, how are you possibly supposed to narrow that down and make a prudent investment choice? You drive a Ford utility; does that mean you should own Ford shares? Or is Tesla the car share for your portfolio? You can't live without your daily Starbucks, but is the Howard Schultz empire going to keep producing money for you in the long term?

If only there was an investment vehicle where you could just own a few shares of each of those companies. An easy-to-buy, one-click purchase where you are diversified across industries, companies and sometimes even countries. Well, my dear readers, you just described an index fund. And I would propose to you that could be exactly how you invest the core of your portfolio.

Index funds: your *core* holding

What exactly is an index fund? An index fund is a type of managed fund or exchange-traded fund (ETF) with a portfolio constructed to match or track the components of a financial market index such as the S&P 500 or the ASX 200. An index managed fund is said to provide broad market exposure, low operating expenses and low portfolio turnover. These funds follow their benchmark index regardless of the state of the markets. The ETF or mutual fund allows you to make an investment in multiple — sometimes hundreds or thousands of — companies with just one purchase by you. As the fund owns all the companies, when you buy shares in the fund you are buying all the companies the fund invests in. So the goal for the index fund is to just match, not beat, the underlying index. This concept is known as benchmarking.

Core and satellite investing

Core and satellite investing is when you have the majority (core) of your portfolio in one diversified holding and then smaller allocations to boost performance or diversification — like satellites roaming around the earth (see figure 5.1). So what should be your core holding in this strategy? You might consider a passive, market-based index fund. Generally, the core part of a portfolio could be around 80–90 per cent of the total portfolio.

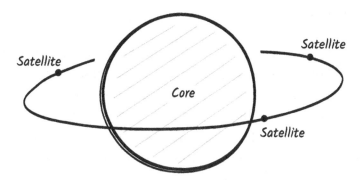

Figure 5.1: core and satellite investing

How index funds work

'Indexing' is a form of passive fund management. Instead of a fund portfolio manager actively share picking and market timing — that is, choosing securities to invest in and strategising when to buy and sell them — the fund manager builds a portfolio whose holdings mirror the securities of a particular index. The idea is that by mimicking the profile of the index — the share market as a whole, or a broad segment of it — the fund will match its performance as well. Essentially, you're investing in the shares of a bunch of companies at once to mitigate risk.

There is an index and an index fund for nearly every financial market in existence. As Glen pointed out earlier, in the United States, the most popular index funds track the S&P 500. But several other indexes are widely used as well, including:

- *the MSCI EAFE Index* — consisting of foreign shares from Europe, Australasia and Asia

- *the ASX 200 Index* — this tracks the top 200 Australian shares

- *the Bloomberg US Aggregate Bond Index* — which follows the total US bond market

- *the NASDAQ Composite Index* — made up of 3000 shares listed on the NASDAQ exchange.

Portfolios of index funds only change substantially when their benchmark indexes change. For instance, the film company Kodak used to be one of the largest companies in the United States and was therefore in the Dow Jones index (DJIA), which is made up of the United States' 30 largest companies. Well, when digital cameras came into fashion, Kodak fell out of the DJIA top 30 and was replaced by a new company.

Since it is the most popular index in the world, let's look at what makes up the S&P 500 index. I use an S&P 500 index as my core holding in both my retirement, taxable brokerage and children's education funds. Why? Well keep reading — this isn't the CliffNotes.

What's in the S&P 500?

This weighted index is composed of 500 of the largest publicly traded companies in the United States, with a wide breadth of exposure to 11 different market sectors. It is market weighted. Take a look at the heat map in figure 5.2, which shows you that some companies have more weight in the average than others. The larger the company, the larger the weight in the index — so Apple, being the largest company in the world according to market capitalisation, is the largest holding in the S&P 500 index.

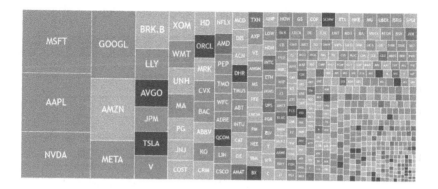

Figure 5.2: this S&P 500 heat map gives you a visual representation of the 500 companies in the index based on size. The larger the company as a part of the index (see MSFT, for example), the larger they are on the map. The smaller the company, the less impact on the index (see BA, for example).
Source: © 2024 TradingView, Inc. Captured 15 May 2024.

Man, that's a lot of companies! But I guess that's the point: by purchasing an S&P 500 index you have the safety of investing in over 500 of the largest companies in the United States. If 20 companies have a bad year, 80 have an okay year and the other 400 do well, then you are going to have a good year for your investments, even with 100 companies doing below average.

So I think index investing specifically in the S&P 500 is a good idea. But what do I know? Let me tell you what my close personal friend, and the greatest investor of all time, has to say: Warren Buffet says to buy an index fund. As an American businessman he particularly likes index funds that track the S&P 500.

But why does the Oracle of Omaha want us to buy the S&P 500? Well, it has a great track record for one: check out table 5.1 (overleaf) for the growth of the S&P 500 over the past five decades.

Table 5.1: how the S&P 500 index has performed since the 1970s, expressed as percentages

Year	Growth
1970s	+77%
1980s	+407%
1990s	+433%
2000s	-9%
2010s	+259%

Investing in the S&P 500 gives you access to all of the 11 industries we introduced in chapter 4 and 500 of the biggest US companies. Investing in an index fund is an easy and stress-free way to invest for most people because you're not betting on one company but the 500 largest American companies. If the S&P 500 goes down, the whole world has bigger issues than your retirement savings dropping.

Australia's version of the S&P 500

Warren Buffett is an American so he might have a bias towards US funds. If you want the Australian counterpart to the S&P 500, look no further than the ASX 200. You can diversify across 200 of Australia's largest companies just as easily with one click of a button when you buy something like the State Street Advisers SPDR S&P/ASX 200 Fund (STW). This fund seeks to closely match, before fees and expenses, the returns of the ASX 200 Index, and you have already learned that there are several investment managers that offer ETFs that invest in the same indexes.

An ASX 200 Index fund will provide you with diversification across 200 companies as well as 11 different sectors. For details, see figure 5.3.

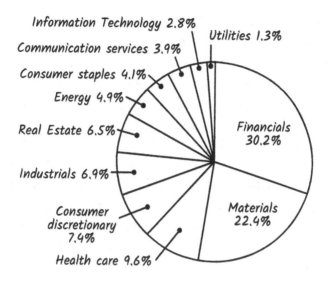

Information Technology 2.8%
Utilities 1.3%
Communication services 3.9%
Consumer staples 4.1%
Energy 4.9%
Real Estate 6.5%
Industrials 6.9%
Consumer discretionary 7.4%
Health care 9.6%
Financials 30.2%
Materials 22.4%

Figure 5.3: the sector breakdown of the ASX200

Investing in action

Take some time to carry out research on either the ASX 200 or the S&P 500. Choose one of these indices, look for one company within the index you recognise and one you don't recognise, and research what each company does.

Index funds vs actively managed funds

Okay, so you get it. Owning shares in a fund with lots of companies diversified over many sectors is a good idea. But my neighbour says that his manager has him in a hot new fund that is beating the market this year. Why not buy an actively managed fund?

One primary advantage that index funds have over their actively managed counterparts is the lower management *expense ratio*. A fund's expense ratio—also known as the management expense ratio (MER)—includes all of the operating expenses, such as the payments for managers, transaction fees, taxes and accounting fees.

Because the index fund managers are simply replicating the performance of a benchmark index, they do not need the services of research analysts and others who assist in the share-selection process. Index fund managers trade holdings less often, incurring fewer transaction fees and commissions. In contrast, actively managed funds have more staff and conduct more transactions, driving up the cost of doing business.

The extra costs of fund management are reflected in the fund's expense ratio and get passed on to investors. As a result, cheap index funds often cost less than 1 per cent: 0.2 per cent to 0.5 per cent is typical. Some firms offer even lower expense ratios of 0.05 per cent or less. Compare that to the much higher fees that actively managed funds command, where, typically, 1 to 2 per cent in US-based funds is common.

Expense ratios directly impact the overall performance of a fund. Actively managed funds, with their often higher expense ratios, are automatically at a disadvantage compared to index funds and struggle to keep up with their benchmarks in terms of overall return.

Advocates argue that passive funds have been successful in outperforming most actively managed mutual funds. Indeed, a majority of mutual funds fail to beat their benchmark or broad market indexes. For instance, during the five-year period ending 31 December 2020, approximately 75 per cent of large-cap US funds generated a return that was less than that of the S&P 500, according to SPIVA Scorecard data from S&P Dow Jones Indexes.

A quick note before moving on: I am not against actively managed funds per se. I am a man who likes the odds on my side. So when many, if not most, of the funds with 2 per cent fees of up to are not beating the market it makes sense to put your hard-earned money on the statistical bet that low-cost index funds will be your best bet.

That being said, there are some money managers that do earn their keep. They are hard to come by and you must do your research—they must prove themselves with a solid track record. Like Peter Lynch, who outperformed the market while producing an average 29 per cent return on the Magellan Fund from 1977 to 1990! But Peter Lynch was head and shoulders above most money managers so now the safe bet with your money might more likely be index fund investing.

Building your portfolio for growth

I'm feeling good about your progress. You've become indoctrinated in the wonderful world of low-cost index investing as the core holding for your portfolio construction. And if that's all you ever invest in, you're doing great and you could stop reading this book now. Go out and get your brokerage account set up with automatic monthly investments and just buy right and sit tight.

But let's assume you want to learn more about investing than just buying an index fund. Well, let's now turn our attention to other smaller holdings to round out your fully allocated portfolio.

The most popular portfolio construction over the past 75 years has been the 60/40 asset allocation. This portfolio holds 60 per cent equities and 40 per cent bonds to create a mix of growth and defensive investments. Historically, this has been thought of as a safe risk-to-reward portfolio in that the bonds might mitigate the risk of the equities in your portfolio.

Personally, as an investor who has lived through the 2000s dot-com bust and invested through the global financial crisis (GFC) of 2008, the downturn of 2018 and the COVID-19 bust of 2020, and finally the 2022 market correction, I have not seen the safety net that the 60/40 portfolio previously seemed to provide.

In 2008, a typical 60/40 share and bond portfolio experienced a significant decline in value, primarily due to the GFC and the severe market turbulence that year. The GFC led to substantial losses in both equity (shares) and fixed income (bond) markets.

In 2008, the S&P 500 index, suffered a sharp decline. The total return for the year, including both price depreciation and dividends, was approximately –37.0 per cent.

Bonds, often seen as a safe haven in times of economic uncertainty, fared better than shares but still faced challenges. The Bloomberg US Aggregate Bond Index, a common benchmark for US investment-grade bonds, had a positive total return of approximately 5.24 per cent for the year. However, while bonds provided a positive return, this was not enough to offset the substantial losses experienced in the share market.

To calculate the return of a 60/40 portfolio for 2008, you might consider blending these two asset classes together:

$$(60\% \times share\ return) + (40\% \times bond\ return) = (0.60 \times -37.0\%)$$
$$+ (0.40 \times 5.24\%) = -22.2\% + 2.096\% = -20.104\%$$

So, a typical 60/40 share and bond portfolio (illustrated in figure 5.4) would have experienced a negative return of approximately –20.10 per cent in 2008. The GFC had a profound impact on investment portfolios during that year, emphasising the importance of asset allocation and risk management in portfolio construction.

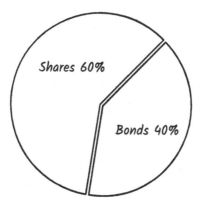

Figure 5.4: a typical 60/40 share and bond portfolio

A more recent snag of the 60/40 portfolio was seen in 2022 when the portfolio returned –16.9 per cent.

As you can see, the 60/40 'safe' portfolio sometimes isn't all that safe. So how should you look at investing for diversification into a portfolio that allows adequate upside with some downside protection?

To be fair, the bond section did hold up its end in 2008 by offsetting the losses of the shares. But I'd put more faith in the historical returns of the share market over the long term than hedging my bet during the most important growth years when you are younger.

So if you are reading this book and looking to start your journey off in investing, and are under the age of 60, I would not be looking into the popular 60/40 portfolio. Time is on your side and you will want to be more fully invested with a larger potential upside of the historical returns of 10 per cent over 20+ years. Through the volatility of ups and downs, if you keep your money invested in the share market you probably don't need the hedge of bonds to protect your portfolio. If anything, the bonds are eating into the potential upside that your share index provides.

Another way advisers have been guiding clients over the years has been to scale up your use of bonds according to your age. This gives you more upside with shares in your younger years and then you gain perceived safety into bonds each year you get older. Do I sound sceptical? That's because I am. But for educational purposes, let's run through a scenario.

This methodology would take 100 minus your age as your share exposure. If you are 25 years old, 25 would be your bond portfolio percentage. So instead of a traditional 60/40 portfolio construction, at 25 years old you would have a 75/25 construction.

Warren Buffet is 93 years old and he doesn't have any bonds in his portfolio. Take that for what it's worth.

So where does all of this leave us? If you want a long-term portfolio to build your wealth with DCA, how should you do that if not with a mix of bonds and shares? That's where the three-fund portfolio comes in.

The three-fund (keep it simple, stupid) portfolio

Perhaps this reflects on my level of intelligence, but my mother used to say, 'keep it simple, stupid', and I remember this often when judging investment decisions. When I get in my head and I start to overthink my investment portfolios, I think of that saying from my dear mum and I keep it simple. Well, at least for the core of my portfolio.

By owning just three mutual funds, or ETFs, you can gain access to thousands of companies and a well-diversified portfolio. Here is the broad scope of what you'll want, no matter where you are in the world:

- a total domestic equity fund

- a total bond fund

- a total international equity fund.

With just these three funds, the average retail investor can outperform the vast majority of actively managed mutual funds available on the market. How can I make the claim that passive index-based funds will most likely outperform active managed funds? We've already covered that in the book, but as a reminder: over the past 20 years 78 per cent of managed funds have failed to beat the index funds.

Not too long ago, I went through this exercise with my sister to help her create her portfolio because she is in charge of making the investments inside of her retirement account from a previous job. She asked me for my advice on what to invest in so we went over the benefits of the simple three-fund portfolio.

My sister works for a REIT. She does not have the time, nor the desire, to be managing her portfolio — or even to be looking at her portfolio, to be honest. In fact, she doesn't really want to think about it much once she's chosen her investments. So I found three total market funds that fit the methodology of the 'keep it simple, stupid', three-fund portfolio. I found her a total US equity fund, a total US bond fund and a total international equity fund.

But enough about my lovely sis. Let's talk about you! Let's imagine an Australian three-fund portfolio holder: let's say, a 30-year-old social media account manager who works and lives in Sydney. They know they need to invest but don't have the time to worry about asset allocation, tactical asset management or even portfolio rebalancing. They have no desire to do much work on their portfolio. Figure 5.5 depicts an option they could look into for their three-fund portfolio.

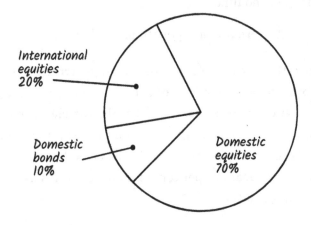

Figure 5.5: an example of a three-fund portfolio, including domestic bonds, international equities and domestic equities

For this example, I chose iShares ETFs, but if you already have a broker or platform, you could choose any similar low-cost, passive, total market fund. Here's what the breakdown could look like:

- *The domestic equities fund might be IOZ: iShares Core S&P/ASX 200 ETF, with a net expense of 0.05 per cent. The top holdings include BHP Group Ltd, CBA, Woodside Energy Group Ltd, Telstra Group Ltd (and so on) and, as the name indicates, this fund shoots to hold 200 of Australia's largest publicly traded companies.*

- *The low cost total domestic bond fund might be IAF: iShares Core Composite Bond ETF with a net expense fee of 0.10 per cent.*

This fund holds mainly Australian treasuries of different maturities in length from zero to one year all the way up to 20-year maturities.

- *The international total market equities fund might be IVV:* this is from BlackRock and it tracks the S&P 500 US index; has a net expense ratio of 0.07 per cent; and has a dividend yield of 1.39 per cent. You would be invested in the top 500 companies in the United States.

So, with a few clicks of a button you could purchase three funds with an average fee of 0.08 per cent and gain access to domestic equities, domestic bonds and a total market international fund.

Then you might set up auto buys and start sending money from your account to your new three-fund investment portfolio each month.

Getting back to what percentage to put into each of the three funds, many in the investment world take the safe approach to rebalancing their portfolio by age: more equities and fewer bonds when you are young; and more bonds and fewer equities as you age.

That is a conservative allocation for my personal take. I think time is on your side and you should be aggressive early on. My sister's new three-fund portfolio is 90 per cent equities and 10 per cent bonds and she is in her early 40s. At the end of the day, you need to make decisions that make you comfortable. To be successful at investing, you need to be as relaxed as possible with your portfolio construction so you are not second-guessing yourself all the time or feeling stressed out.

Remember: there are countless brokerage accounts, platforms and apps to choose from and all of these have access to these types of low-cost, total-market type funds. The goal is to pick one, set it up and get invested as soon as you can, making it an automatic habit each month to build wealth for your future self.

You want more simple?

Is picking three index funds too much for you to think about? Then you might want to look at our next option of easy, one-click diversification: diversified ETFs. As Glen mentioned in chapter 3, these kinds of funds provide low-cost access across multiple asset classes. They are ETFs that buy and blend other ETFs to give you ownership of hundreds, and maybe thousands, of companies across sectors and sometimes countries.

As the name indicates, one of the major advantages in a diversified ETF is, well, diversification. While many investors understand not putting all your eggs in one basket, this takes that thought a step further. For example, many investors might invest in the ASX 200 and that does diversify you across different companies in Australia. But it only diversifies you within the Australian market, whereas a fund like the Vanguard Diversified High Growth (VDHG) Index ETF, or the Betashares Diversified All Growth (DHHF) ETF, will give you share ownership of diversified Australian and global companies. Beyond the benefits of one-stop diversification, these ETFs offer rebalancing for you as well. If you want a hands-off approach to investing, take a look at a sample of the Vanguard VDHG in table 5.2.

So, by investing in this one Vanguard fund you would have access to 90 per cent growth of domestic, global and emerging markets, as well as 10 per cent fixed income and bonds. Like the name says, it's well diversified.

Table 5.2: the Vanguard VDHG holdings

Asset allocation	%
Growth assets	
Vanguard Aus Shares Index Fund	35.8
Vanguard Int. Shares Index Fund	26.6
Vanguard Int. Shares Index Fund Hedged	16
Vanguard Int. Small Comp Index Fund	6.5
Vanguard Emerging Market Index Shares Fund	4.9
Total growth	*89.8*
Income assets	
Vanguard Global Agg Bond Index Fund	7.2
Vanguard Australian Fixed Interest Index Fund	3
Total income	*10.2*
Total	*100*

Source: Vanguard.

Life stage / target date fund investing

If you want diversification that changes with you according to your life stage and age in one click of a button, then LifeStage investment options — also known as target-date or age-based investment options — might be for you. They are a common feature in superannuation accounts. These options are designed to automatically adjust the asset allocation of your investments based on your age or expected retirement date. The primary goal is to optimise your portfolio's risk and return profile to align with your changing financial needs and risk tolerance as you approach retirement.

Here's how LifeStage investment options work:

- *Initial allocation.* When you first start investing in a LifeStage option, your portfolio typically has a higher allocation to growth assets such as shares and real estate. This is because younger investors can generally afford to take on more risk for the potential of higher returns. The initial allocation is often determined based on the target retirement year associated with the fund.

- *Automatic rebalancing.* As you get closer to your target retirement date, the fund will automatically adjust its asset allocation to become more conservative. This means reducing the exposure to riskier assets like shares and increasing allocations to more conservative investments like bonds and cash. The objective is to reduce the impact of market volatility on your investments as you near retirement.

- *Prebuilt-in diversification.* LifeStage funds are typically well-diversified across various asset classes and geographic regions. This diversification helps spread risk and can provide a level of stability, even as the asset allocation changes.

- *Hands-off approach.* LifeStage options are designed to be hands-off, meaning you don't need to actively manage your asset allocation as you age. The fund manager takes care of this automatically, which can be beneficial for investors who prefer a more passive investment approach.

- *Continual monitoring.* The fund manager continually monitors and adjusts the asset allocation to ensure it aligns with the fund's investment strategy and objectives. They may also make adjustments based on market conditions and economic outlook.

The one potential drawback of LifeStage options is that they may not perfectly align with your individual financial situation and risk tolerance as they are click-and-buy based on your age, not your true risk tolerance. Additionally, the fees associated with these funds can be higher compared to passively managed index funds.

It's important to note that not all LifeStage funds are created equal: the specific asset allocation changes and investment strategy can vary among fund providers. It's essential to carefully review the fund's prospectus and consider your individual financial goals and risk tolerance before choosing a LifeStage investment option within your superannuation account. If you have concerns or specific preferences, you may also want to consult with a financial adviser for guidance on selecting the right option for your retirement savings. But if you are looking for the simplest one-stop shop with built-in diversification and not much maintenance needed, LifeStage funds are possibly for you.

If, however, you want to be a more hands-on investor — someone who likes the sound of a core portfolio of a broad-based index fund but then gets to pick and choose satellite investments to help supplement that core ETF — well, read on my friends because in the next chapters we will get into single shares and advanced investing strategies that you might be interested in.

Start with this ...

Let's end the chapter by taking a good look at your soon-to-be
or current portfolio.

* Check your superannuation account. Are you in a life-stage
  default fund? (This may have your birth decade in the
  name of the investment option.) If yes, are you happy with
  this after what you have learned?

* Does your portfolio follow one of the examples laid out in
  this chapter? Are you an index investor or do you have
  active funds? Are you a core/satellite investor? Are you a
  three-fund investor? Are you a one-stop-shop investor?

* Now that you've identified what kind of investor you are,
  is this the type of investor you want to be? If not, maybe
  re-read this chapter, see what type fits your personality and
  lifestyle the most and, if warranted, make some changes
  so that your investing style matches your ability and
  your desires.

6

Build your portfolio: single shares investing

(Nick)

I love the outdoors. I grew up in Alaska and every weekend during my high school years and university I was out in the wilderness. I loved everything: backpacking, mountain biking and especially hiking big mountains. There are countless mountains to hike in Alaska. After a while, I decided to combine my love of travelling with hiking. The first international mountain I hiked was Mount Fuji in Japan. Fuji then led to a trip to Mount Kilimanjaro in Kenya and then to the tallest and toughest mountain to date: Cerro Aconcagua in Argentina. Aconcagua is the tallest mountain in South America and in fact the highest in the Western hemisphere.

What I've learned from hiking these mountains is that more effort goes into preparing for the climb than actually doing the climb. By the time you take your first step up a mountain, especially a big mountain, you've already climbed it in your head 100 times. You've put in long hikes on other mountains to prepare your legs. You've studied maps and maps and maps on maps. You've purchased gear, tested the gear and packed it all neatly away in a large backpack. Before you go out and hike a big mountain you know that mountain intimately.

Similarly, before you go out and buy shares in a company, you need to know that company. Buying single shares is an upfront endeavour—you'll need to do most of your work before buying anything. Do the research beforehand and you'll make the most informed decisions you can, giving you the greatest chance at investing success.

The previous chapter should have equipped you with all the tools you need to master the art of portfolio construction. You may now have selected a three-fund portfolio, a core and satellite approach, or a LifeStage fund inside your superannuation (but we would question your decision with a LifeStage fund lol). In this chapter we are going to focus our attention on what it takes to invest in single shares. Then we'll take a peek at what we can learn from some of the best share pickers in the industry.

Keep in mind that for the average person who wants to invest but who would not call themselves an 'investor', Glen and I do not think single shares should make up more than 5 to 10 per cent of a portfolio. It's fun to get creative and see if you can help expand the performance of your index-based portfolio by selecting individual shares with that 5 to 10 per cent. But word to the wise—and that's you since you are reading this book—be cautious and do your research. And good luck as you try to find the next Apple, Tesla or Monster Energy!

We explained why we believe index investing should be your primary holding earlier in the book, but if you skipped to this chapter here's a quick recap.

Index funds provide instant diversification by holding a broad range of shares, bonds or other assets that make up the index they track. This diversification helps spread risk and reduces the impact of poor performance in any single share. Why try and bet on the next Tesla EV start-up when you can buy, let's say, a NASDAQ ETF with a wide range of companies that will benefit from the overall market capitalisation of electric vehicles? Investing in individual shares can be risky because the value of one company can rise and fall significantly. Index funds mitigate this risk since they represent a basket of companies or assets, reducing the impact of any one company's performance on your overall investment. Even the greatest investor of all time, Warren Buffet, says for the average person a broad-based index fund is the go when investing. He specifically likes the S&P 500 because you own the top 500 US-based companies with one click of the buy button.

With that being said—and with that important disclaimer out of the way—yes, Warren Buffet tells you to buy the index fund and that it is the best bet for *you*. But he doesn't do that for himself or for Berkshire Hathaway, the investment company that he ran with the late Charlie Munger. In fact, in 1996, when speaking to an audience at the annual Berkshire Hathaway investors meeting, Buffet said this about diversification:

Diversification is a protection against ignorance, if you wanna make sure that nothing bad happens to you relative to the market, you own everything. There is nothing wrong with that, that is a perfectly sound approach for someone who doesn't know how to analyse businesses.

Read that quote carefully. Do you know how to analyse a business? Can you properly value a business by reading its financial statements? If so, you can skip this chapter. If not, maybe keep reading and we'll see if there's something to Buffet's statement.

Warren Buffet tells the average investor who is not invested in doing their own research that they should simply buy an index fund and match the market. And I agree ... to a point. But if you are reading this chapter, it's possible you're interested in investing and doing your own research. So for you, the interested party, there's a chance you could be a share picker, at least with a portion of your portfolio.

If that's you, I want you to imagine you're investing in individual shares that could outpace the market (because I'm sure you've heard many times that finding a share to beat the market is like finding a needle in a haystack). Yes, it can be difficult, but a needle in a haystack makes it seem more like winning the lottery than doing some due diligence.

Let's look at 2023 and see how difficult it was to beat the market with individual shares. If you've paid attention to the share-market news over the past decade or so, you might have heard of FAANG stocks. Before FAANG it was the Nifty Fifty, and in 2023 everyone dropped FAANG and started talking about the Magnificent Seven (or Mag7). This was a group of seven stocks that the news said was driving the entire market's performance. In 2023, the Mag7 was similar to FAANG, with a few swaps. See table 6.1.

Table 6.1: comparing FAANG to the Mag7 and showing the differences

FAANG	Mag7
Facebook	Facebook
Apple	Apple
Amazon	Amazon
Netflix	Nvidia
Google	Google
	Microsoft
	Tesla

Because the S&P is a weighted index, these seven stocks did help drive a lot of the performance for the S&P 500 in 2023. But does that mean the other 493 stocks were down and dragging the index down with them? See table 6.2 for a snapshot of the top 10 shares in the S&P 500 in 2023.

Table 6.2: the top 10 shares in the S&P 500 in 2023

Share	Return
NVIDIA (NVDA)	236%
Meta (META)	193.4%
Royal Caribbean (RCL)	163.4%
Builders Firstsource (BLDR)	157.3%
UBER (UBER)	148.2%
Carnival (CCL)	132.9%
AMD (AMD)	128.2%
PulteGroup (PHM)	126.7%
Palo Alto Networks (PANW)	110.5%
Tesla (TSLA)	102%

All 10 shares in figure 6.2 beat the market by a hefty percentage. Notice that only three of these top 10 are in the Mag7. Some of these companies don't seem all that magnificent but still managed to have great returns. If we had room to expand this chart you would have to get down to number 143 to finally get to a share that just matched the S&P 500. And you would have to go all the way down to number 200 to reach a stock that hit the average of the S&P 500 at 10 per cent per year. Then, nearing share #300 — Starbucks — you'd finally find the break-even or 0 per cent for the year. So it wasn't just the Mag7 driving all returns: 325 shares in the 500 made money; 143 beat the S&P 500; and only 175 were negative or flat for the year. So, in 2023 you had a 40 per cent chance of at least matching the market return. That's a pretty big needle.

How to value a company

Now let's find out what some of the top money managers look for when valuing a company and see if we can't make single share investing an even more approachable goal for individual investors — that's us!

We're going to discover some helpful hints on how to value and analyse a business so that if you'd like to have some single shares in your portfolio you can be a knowledgeable business owner — because that's exactly what you're doing when you buy single shares: you're buying a piece of a business. Much like you wouldn't buy a car wash or burger franchise without looking into the numbers, you should not buy single shares of a company without doing your research.

Let's go back to the Oracle of Omaha himself, Warren Buffet. There is a great deal of information out there on how Warren and the late Charlie (I hope I can call them by their first names, like we are mates) chose specific companies to add into their portfolio at Berkshire Hathaway.

Lessons from some GOATs

Warren Buffet isn't shy about disclosing that he was an avid student of Benjamin Graham (known as the 'father of value investing'), who focused on quantitative methods. Graham didn't care what a company did in terms of the product or service it sold. He only cared about the numbers: that was his 'cigar-butt' method of value investing. He wanted to find undervalued companies — just as you would find a cigar on the side of the street with a little smoke still left in it — smoke all he could out of them and move on.

Buffett started investing this way too. However, after meeting and working with the late great Charlie Munger he changed his method and focused more on qualitative aspects such as intrinsic value and margin of safety.

Buffett says the three most important words in investing are 'margin of safety'. The margin of safety that Buffett looks for is the difference between the intrinsic value of a share and its market price. Finding the market price of a share is simple enough, but what about its intrinsic value? In *The Theory of Investment Value*, John Burr Williams writes:

> *The intrinsic value of any stock, bond or business today is determined by the cash inflows and outflows, discounted at an appropriate interest rate, that can be expected to occur during the remaining life of that asset.*

Boiled down from that quote, intrinsic value is the present value of all future cash flows added together. This means you need to know how much cash the business will make in the future and what those future cash flows are worth to you today.

Buffett often uses the analogy of buying a farm to explain intrinsic value. If you were to buy a farm, you would be interested in its long-term earning potential, the quality of its soil, the competence of its management and other factors that contribute to its future cash flows. Similarly, when Buffett assesses a company, he looks at its fundamentals, such as earnings, dividends, growth potential and the competitive advantage it has in its industry.

Buffett's approach to intrinsic value involves estimating the future cash flows a business will generate and discounting them back to their present value. This discounted cash flow (DCF) analysis helps him determine the intrinsic value of a company.

Famous investor Peter Lynch of the Magellan Fund at Fidelity believed in picking shares one by one after thorough research rather than expecting a speculative platform to throw open a list of 'good shares'. Instead, take one share at a time and get acquainted with the company and the industry. He observed that before people buy a car, they read and learn about the car; before they buy a TV, they research and compare TVs; yet when they buy stocks they listen to the next hot pick from a stranger. When you do that, you should not be surprised when it goes down because you didn't really know what you were investing in.

So let's examine some advice from the godfather of Fidelity and try to make Peter Lynch proud. I want you to know how to value a company that you are considering buying shares in as well as you know the menu at your favourite Thai food joint.

Perhaps you've heard from your favourite podcaster (no, not Glen, me!) that you need to do your homework before you buy a share. But what does that mean? The phrase 'Do your homework' is about as helpful as directions from a person who speaks in north, south, east and west. If I ask you for directions (not sure why I would be asking a real, live human being — maybe my phone battery is dead?), I need to be told, 'Take a right at the petrol station and a left at the shopping centre'. When you give me directions, use right and left, not north and south. I'm not a 14th century naval navigator!

Anyway, let's figure out what to look for when we are 'doing our homework', aka when researching any shares out there that we may want to buy for our investing portfolios.

Both Peter Lynch and Warren Buffet, and for that matter any long-term investor worth their salt, would tell you to not invest in a company if you can't *explain* how it makes money. Think about it this way: if you want to buy a house, you are going to do lots of research. You are going to look at the numbers: How big is it?; How many bedrooms and bathrooms does it have ...? Then you will check the price, and maybe the price per square metre, and compare it to other similar homes. You'd check the schooling zones, council rates and any strata fees, if applicable. If a potential house comes in at a huge discount by the standards of the area, there's probably a reason for it — and potentially not a good one. It might be the right size, have the right number of bedrooms and be within your price range, but then you find out it's in the wrong schooling zone — and that makes it no good for you.

Same thing applies to shares. Just because a share seems cheap compared to its competition, or the price-to-earnings (P/E) ratio is under 20 (more on P/E soon) doesn't mean it is a company worth buying. You want to look at the entire business before buying into the business.

That's where understanding the business model and the market in which the company operates comes into play. Do some quick research of the management and then dig into the actual numbers of the company and make sure it is a profitable and healthy business.

Understanding the basic business model

As an investor, you should at all costs avoid buying an individual share of a company unless you have knowledge of its basic business model. There are four questions to ask yourself about the company:

1. What does it manufacture?

2. Who is its target market?

3. Is it diversified in product offerings or is it a one-trick pony?

4. Is it reliant upon a great economy or well propped up to thrive in all types of business cycles?

Answering these four basic questions can help you identify whether you understand the company.

Company management

Warren Buffet once said about hiring people — and when you buy a share you are essentially hiring the CEO — that you want to learn how they hire, how they lead and where they want the company to go.

Proper company management is an important factor to consider when investing long term in a company. If you are making a day trade or a swing trade (these types of trade are discussed in chapter 8), you don't need to be digging so deep into a company. If, however, you are looking to invest in single shares over a long-term (7+ years) timeframe, then company management matters. A good CEO can provide profit or sink companies.

But don't be discouraged: you don't need to interview a top CEO to figure out the management style. Do an internet search of the company to find the CEO. Then search the CEO and look for red flags like job skipping, trouble with the law, unethical practices and so on. Has the company just hired a new CEO? Typically, current investors will let you know what they think about that decision. Look back at the date the CEO was hired and see if the share price popped or dropped the day after the announcement. Look at Disney in 2022 when it announced that Bob Iger was returning as CEO. Disney shares shot up 10 per cent in pre-market trading and ended the day up 6.3 per cent all because investors were happy with the decision to re-hire Iger.

Many famous investors like to invest in companies that are founder driven. When someone is the founder of the company and the company is profitable for years on end, it is likely that the drive and vision from those profits are related to the founder's vision being played out.

Steve Jobs was the co-founder and visionary leader of Apple. However, once Apple became a publicly traded company his big vision, according to the board, began getting in the way of significant profits. In 1983 Jobs hired former Pepsi CEO John Sculley. This hire ended up accelerating Jobs being let go two years later. Sculley and the board wanted to go one way with product launch and design and Steve Jobs wanted to go another drastically different way.

So, in 1985 the board removed Jobs from the company he co-founded.

Jobs then founded NeXT, a high-end computer company. NeXT was never a huge success, but with Jobs off the job at Apple it wasn't succeeding well either. Apple ended up buying NeXT for $429 million USD. Steve Jobs was placed into the CEO role at Apple ... and the rest is history.

Are all founder-led companies successful? No. But if you find ones that have a track record of profitability and a good-looking plan for the future, you're likely to have found one that outperforms its non-founder-led peers.

Investing in action

Before we learn more about how to research companies, let's practise investigating a company's current CEO. Choose a well-known company, or one you like, and do some online research about the current CEO. Look for information regarding the future they envisage for the company, what they look for when hiring, how their appointment as CEO affected share performance and any issues or red flags in their previous behaviour.

Six key investment ratios

Okay, you've reviewed the basics of the company and dug into the management (this should have been easy and quick to do if you have Google available). Next, it would be helpful to really dig down into the financials of the company. And don't get too scared with this prospect. There are many helpful websites where you can find this information and I'm about to teach you the basics of some key financial ratios to look at to compare one company with another.

Of course, none of these ratios guarantee the share will perform the way you expect it to, but knowing these six investment ratios will help you identify shares you may want to buy and hold in your portfolio. I will outline how you can run these numbers yourself. Many financial websites have already run the equation and posted the figure for you, but read my explanations as a way to familiarise yourself with what these numbers mean in the real world. After all, you will be investing real money into real companies to get a real return.

These are the six key investment ratios that I'm going to describe for you:

1. Price-to-free-cash-flow

2. Price-to-sales

3. EPS earnings per share

4. Return on invested capital (ROIC)

5. Price-to-earnings

6. Dividend yield.

Price-to-free-cash-flow ratio

Price-to-free-cash-flow is a favourite ratio for dividend investors, particularly those investing in utility and commodity companies such as energy plants or drilling sites, which incur high operating expenses.

Free cash flow is how much money a company has after it pays the bills. By subtracting a company's operating expenses, and other expenses used to buy or upgrade assets like buildings and equipment, you are left with free cash flow.

To determine the price-to-free-cash-flow ratio, divide the company's market capitalisation by its free cash flow. Or you can divide its share price by its cash flow per share if you have that figure handy.

For example, Australian mining company BHP Group's share price is $61.47 and its free cash flow per share trailing 12 months was $12.60. As such, BHP's price-to-free-cash-flow ratio is 4.87.

A lower ratio indicates a company may be undervalued, while a higher ratio may signal overvaluation. Historically, investors like to see a ratio under 10. The lower the number, the 'better' the value of the share.

Price-to-sales ratio (P/S)

The price-to-sales ratio (P/S) is also known as a sales multiple or revenue multiple. The market agrees that the lower the P/S of a company, the better value you are getting as a shareholder because you are paying less for every dollar of a company's revenue. Contrastingly, the higher the ratio, the more you are paying per dollar of revenue. So a lower P/S is good for you; a higher P/S is good for the company.☺

To figure out the P/S ratio, divide the share price by sales per share. Or you can calculate the company's market cap divided by its total sales.

Like all ratios, the P/S makes most sense when you are comparing companies in the same industry. You would expect a tech company and an energy company to have wildly different P/E ratios, so there's no point in comparing apples with oranges.

Earnings-per-share (EPS) ratio

You buy a share in a company because you want the value of the price per share to go up in the future. One of the main determinants for a share to rise over time is good earnings for the company. So, a valuable metric for measuring the potential growth of a share is the EPS because when you buy shares, you participate in the future earnings as well as the potential of missed earnings and therefore share depreciation. EPS is a measure of the profitability of a company. As a long-term investor you will use it to find out for yourself the potential value of a company.

The good news for you is that the company's analysts calculate EPS for you and the number will be readily posted on most financial websites. They calculate it by dividing net income by the weighted average number of common shares outstanding during the year:

Net Income / Weighted Average = Earnings Per Share

The EPS can be zero or negative if a company has no earnings or negative earnings, representing a loss. You want to see a high EPS because the higher the EPS, the greater the value of your shares.

Return on invested capital (ROIC) ratio

ROIC can sound complicated, but it doesn't have to be. Money has a cost to it, either loaned from a bank or acquired through the sale of shares. The capital or money a company acquires costs it something. So the way it deploys that capital needs to exceed the cost of the capital for it to be a good, profitable company. Can it earn high returns on the capital it is given? That's what the ROIC tells you.

When reviewing a company's ROIC you want to see that it was able to borrow at, let's say, 5 per cent and generate 15 per cent on that borrowed money, for a 10 per cent return on capital spread.

When talking about ROIC, Charlie Munger said, in 'A Lesson on Elementary, Worldly Wisdom As It Relates to Investment Management & Business' (5 May 1995):

> It's hard for a stock to earn a much better return than the business which underlies it earns. If the business earns 6% on capital over 40 years ... you're not going to make much more than a 6% return — even if you originally buy it at a huge discount.

Price-to-earnings (P/E) ratio

The P/E ratio, as you will usually see it written or hear it said, is helpful to know when you are trying to find value in a share. The P/E ratio is used as a metric to compare the price of this share vs the price of another share, as well as how much you are willing to pay for a share of a company now for future earnings.

Let's consider 10 years of the S&P 500: March 2013 to March 2023. The P/E ratio for the index as a whole ranged from a low of 17.66 to a high of 39.99. Overall, the index of the largest 500 companies in the United States averaged a P/E of around 21.

If a company has a P/E of 21, that means investors are willing to pay $21 for every dollar of generated revenue of the company. So if you are buying shares in a company, you want to be fairly confident it has plans for future growth.

While many investors focus on the P/E ratio to determine whether a share is cheap or good value, many great investors focus on whether the company can make money on its money and whether it lets the share price work itself out over the long term. The P/E ratio can help you make good short-term purchases. The ROIC helps identify whether that purchase was of a good business.

$$ROIC = (Net\ Income - Dividends)\ /\ (Debt + Equity)$$

Dividend yield ratio

The dividend yield ratio is not the most important investment number but probably is my favourite. I love it when my money makes money, and when you purchase shares of a dividend company you have the potential upside growth of the company in terms of share price as well as the dividend payout from the free cash flows of the company. Most companies pay out the dividend once a quarter, but many companies, like REITs, pay out monthly dividends.

Almost every broker — even the Apple share app by *Yahoo Finance* — will show you the 'Div Yield', but if you want to figure it out yourself it is calculated using the following formula:

$$Dividend\ Yield = (Current\ Share\ Price\ /\ Annual\ Dividends\ per\ Share) \times 100$$

If a company pays an annual dividend of \$2 per share and the current share price is \$40, the dividend yield would be calculated as follows:

$$Dividend\ Yield = (\$2\ /\ \$40) \times 100 = 5\%$$

How I invest in single shares

All of the above information is important. Now let me boil it down on a personal level to demonstrate how I invest in single shares for my long-term portfolio.

I look for high-quality companies. I add them to my portfolio only if they fit a certain criteria. Compared to an index, my portfolio is more concentrated yet still diverse enough for my risk profile. I define the best businesses as ones that have strong, almost monopolistic positions. Warren Buffett calls this 'moat'. I want companies that have high barriers to entry, are popular brand names that I know and like, have cash-rich balance sheets, can scale, have strong organic revenue and have pricing with predictably high returns. These businesses are more often than not gatekeepers and industry leaders. They are the top companies in their industries and therefore their returns are more predictable and repeatable. Here are my tips for picking single shares.

Invest in companies you know and like

I don't always invest in companies I like, but I do start my selection process with ones I like. To go from a company I personally like to a company I buy, that company has to flow through a few other value-based metrics as well (see below). Companies that I like include Apple, Google, Costco, Amazon, Chipotle, Uber, Airbnb, Microsoft, Mastercard, Visa ... and more. What companies do you like as a consumer? Perhaps ones that you use daily or weekly? That could be a starting point for your watch list.

Buy high-quality companies and focus on long-term durable earnings and cash-flow growth

This may seem obvious, and it may also seem like everyone is doing this, but many investors take the six key investing ratios but put most of their focus on the P/E ratio alone. They still use the cigar-butt method, like Benjamin Graham did. This is fine, and it works — it just isn't the same thing as buying shares in high-quality companies while focusing on long-term durable earnings.

P/E talks about the price of a company, but as we know, price isn't everything. A Ford car is going to be cheaper than a Ferrari. That doesn't mean it is better.

Many investors, especially value investors who try to follow Warren Buffet or Peter Lynch, are focused on the multiples a company is trading at. The buying decision is based on the short-term P/E multiple and not the long term. You will remember from my discussion about P/E that under 20 is deemed a good value, but that doesn't mean it's a good buy for your portfolio.

As I mentioned earlier, once Buffett started working with Munger, he changed from cigar-butt mentality to a forward-EPS mentality. He often said at Berkshire Hathway annual meetings that it's better to buy a great company at a reasonable price than a reasonable company at a great price.

So, in both Berkshire Hathaway's portfolio and my personal portfolio and watch list there are companies trading at higher multiples than other shares out there, because I sometimes buy companies that are more expensive if I am basing my value off the next 12 months' earnings per share. I try to have a longer term EPS outlook — again, this is because I prioritise the quality of the company along with earnings and cash-flow growth.

When you look at the chart in figure 6.1, you can see that over the past 25 years the EPS has been driving the price of a share, not the P/E ratio (multiple expansion, or buying low and selling high). The P/E is more of a short-term strategy while the EPS is more long term.

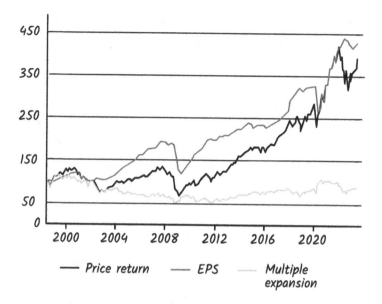

Figure 6.1: how the S&P 500 creates value
Sourced from: Macquarie, Macrobond, Factset, S&P Global.

This clicked for me when I changed my philosophy of buying a stock because it was cheap (according to the P/E ratio) and I started looking for and buying shares in companies that have proven to compound their earnings year-on-year. I call these companies compounders. This is known as looking for and buying 'compounders'. Buying companies that are great long term buying that will compound earnings year-on-year.

When looking for a compounder, I aim for the following:

- *return on capital invested:* 20 per cent

- *gross margin:* above 55 per cent

- *operating profit margin:* above 20 per cent

- *cash conversion:* above 85 per cent — the more above 85 per cent it is, the better

- *interest cover* — a debt and profitability ratio used to determine how a company can pay interest on its debt. I like to see a ratio of more than 10, indicating that the company can pay its debts easily.

To find interest cover, look at the company's financials, find the EBIT (earnings before interest and tax) and divide it by the interest expense. For example:

COST (Costco):

> *EBIT 9 248 000/571 000 (interest expense)* = 16.19

Costco meets the threshold of being over 10 so it fits this criteria.

Most of these markers for both this compounder list and the six financial ratios can be found on websites such as *Yahoo Finance*, or a share screening website such as finviz.com.

Company shares aren't always cheap, so buy them when they are

Because compounder companies are more often than not gatekeepers and industry leaders, they are not cheap with regard to their P/E, but over the long haul they should prove to be great investments. Every once in a while you will be presented with a buying opportunity to scoop up a company on your watchlist for a lower-than-the usual P/E ratio, and you should be ready to buy when that opportunity presents itself.

I still find it hard to figure out when to wait for the share price to dip and when to dollar cost average into shares. Typically, when the media is calling for a recession I have to fight the urge to hold cash and wait. For example, during the entire 2023 investing year the media was calling for the recession that never came and many people left great buying opportunities on the sidelines.

Look for dip buying opportunities

When I look to add a company to my portfolio from my watchlist, because it has hit all the criteria, I typically just buy an allotment and then hold some cash back and wait for a dip in price. So, if I want to buy $10 000 of a company, I might buy half today to get started and then look to add the other $5000 on a dip.

Many dips happen within a day or so after a company reports earnings. Even when a company has good earnings the stock will often fluctuate. So being ready to buy after quarterly earnings is something to look for. The dip I'm looking for might be if the share price falls to the 50-day moving average (MA). To find the 50MA, go to your favourite finance website, pull up the chart and select the 50MA indicator. Come hell or high water, if a share on my watchlist falls to the 200-day MA I will borrow money from my neighbours, cousins—little sister if I have to—to add into a position I am confident is a good buy.

So what do you think? Are you ready to be a single shares investor? If you are like me you'll want to be. I mean, who doesn't want to beat the market returns or find the next Netflix, Tesla or Monster Energy with 1000 per cent returns? This is also a personality discussion and about knowing yourself. At the time of printing, Glen does not hold more than two individual shares and it is not a large allocation of his portfolio. He knows his personality can't handle this type investing, even as satellites to his core.

Is finding great single shares investments easy? No, but it is not as hard as you might think. Sticking to your investing plan when things are going down, or second guessing yourself after 12 or 18 months of mediocre returns, is the real difficulty. Honestly, it is likely that pressure to be invested in the next big thing, or pressure to invest outside your rules and 'earn your money', could be why most investment managers consistently fail to beat the average market return.

In the next chapter I'm going to walk you through a slightly different alternative for picking shares to invest in. Rather than digging into each individual company you're considering investing in at a micro level, thematic investing is one slight step higher. It involves taking a more macro perspective by investing in companies that fit specific themes. Hang around and I'll explain it in more depth.

Start with this ...

So, we've really dipped into some detail in this chapter. Let's recap:

∗ Do you think investing in single/individual shares of a company is something that interests you? Are you prepared to do the research?

∗ What sources of information will you use to research the companies you might consider investing in? Build some frameworks around how you will do your research.

∗ How will you approach your own core and satellite investing method? What do you think will fit nicely into your core and what will be your satellites?

∗ Can you remember the six metrics for assessing the performance of a company? Practise assessing them.

∗ What will be your guidelines for choosing which companies to invest in? Refer back to the guidelines I like to use and determine whether any are relevant to you.

7

Thematic investing

Thematic investing has gained prominence in recent years as an alternative approach to traditional investment strategies. This method of investing revolves around identifying, understanding and capitalising on long-term societal and economic trends — typically macro-economic ones (think: 'big picture'). Investors, instead of solely focusing on individual companies or industries, build portfolios around overarching themes or macro trends, aiming to profit from the potential growth and impact of these themes on the global economy. In this chapter we will delve into the concept of thematic investing: its benefits, its challenges and how you as an investor can leverage this strategy to your advantage.

Understanding thematic investing

Thematic investing involves identifying and investing in companies that are poised to benefit from specific trends, themes or disruptive innovations. These themes can encompass a wide range of sectors and industries: from technology and healthcare to environmental sustainability and demographic shifts. By focusing on thematic investing, investors aim to tap into the long-term drivers of change and growth in the global economy.

Don't be intimidated by the above paragraphs. Start by thinking about the years 2020 to 2023. Think about big, large meta events that were happening that you could have (and probably wished you had) invested in due to global or national events. That's the thought process around thematic investing. What huge things are happening in the world? Is it too late, too early or just the right time to make money on these events? What companies, sectors, nations and commodities might get a boost from these events being broadcast all over the news?

In 2023, the huge theme of the year was artificial intelligence (AI). It seemed like every CEO, on every earnings call, was somehow trying to mention the buzz term 'AI' as much as possible. Companies like NVIDIA, Meta (which owns and operates Facebook and Instagram), Google, Microsoft, and others, all had very good stock performance because of their companies' varying stories about how they were using AI to disrupt some aspect of the future. If you invested in nearly any company with a solid AI base in 2023 you probably made money.

So AI was the theme of 2023, but how did each of these companies use AI to make their share money and what should you have been looking for to capitalise on it with them? Well, in general, coming off a bad-performing 2022, the stock market was looking for a good story to sell. Since the stock market is forward looking, a technology like AI could be a story to buy into now as it will help make businesses more efficient in the future. With investors looking for any good story to invest in, they found their golden nugget in the AI craze.

Facebook used AI technology to partially help get past ad blockers set up by Apple and other companies trying to eliminate cookies from their customers. This use boosted Meta's stock to new all-time highs.

NVIDIA builds the GPUs (graphic processing units) that feed the processing power AI needs to do all the tasks we ask it to do. So naturally their share performance soared.

Google and Microsoft each developed AI chatbots, which use natural language processing to create human-like dialogue — again, driving their shares to all-new highs.

You see, there were many different ways to invest in AI and still make lots and lots of money. The theme was AI. You picked the company that best suited your portfolio.

As I said, 2022 was generally a bad year for shares around the world, but there were a few themes to take advantage of if you had an appetite for risk. Due to the invasion of Ukraine by Russian forces, the pipeline from Russia to most EU countries came to a standstill. This caused non-Russian oil and natural gas shares to have a very good performing year. Seven of the top 10 performing shares around the world were involved in oil or natural gas, all achieving over 90 per cent in a year when the S&P 500 dropped –18 per cent.

Had you picked up some shares of EOG Resources (EOG): 139 per cent; Marathon Petroleum (MPC): 122 per cent; ConocoPhillips (COP): 105 per cent; Coterra Energy (COTER): 96 per cent; or Devon Energy (DVN): 93 per cent, you would have been a very happy investor while the rest of the world panicked at their falling portfolios.

Many shares around the globe had a big year in 2021 and there were a few themes to pick and choose from, but two floated to the top of the pile:

- meme stocks (stocks that gain cult-like popularity on social media)

- COVID-19 vaccine manufacturers.

Moderna and Pfizer were both major COVID-19 manufacturers and were great investments to have in your portfolio in 2021. With the entire world and governments pouring money into getting as many vaccines as possible into the arms of the public, there was a huge yearly cash cow for Moderna and Pfizer. Many companies were trying to get their vaccines to be the first, so picking the right winners was a bit tricky, but spreading a little bit of money to each of the top five companies would have been a solid solution.

As good as the performance was for COVID-19 vaccine manufacturers, the nearly bankrupt meme stocks led the way in 2021. Retail traders or investors — if you want to be so bold as to call a meme stock an investment — poured their hard-earned money into violently volatile shares such as AMC, Bed Bath and Beyond, Nokia and, the king of them all and the one that started it all, GameStop.

GameStop started the whole craze, mainly led by one YouTuber and Reddit contributor going by the name of Roaring Kitty. His videos about contributions on the WallStreetBets thread gathered a huge following in an attempt to bring down the hedge funds betting against the little beatdown, GameStop. This was a fascinating story and now there is an entertaining movie out about it called *Dumb Money*. GameStop started in 2021 at $4.75, hitting an all-time intra-day high of $483 and ended the year up 687 per cent!

Now that you have a better grasp of what thematic investing is, I'm sure you can guess that in 2020 a major theme of investing was influenced by the stay-at-home orders from the COVID-19 pandemic. Companies based around our need to be at home for weeks and months at a time made an outsized return.

The theme of stay-at-home investing covered many different sectors in the market. Company shares of Peloton (an at-home stationary bike company) were up 434 per cent, while shares from Zoom (a video communications company) were up 396 per cent. But when you are at home it isn't all work and exercise — some of us wanted to veg out and ignore our problems. As a result, Netflix and other streaming networks were profiting hand over fist as well.

Investing in action

Let's take a moment to consider some megatrends in history that could have affected share performance. I want you to go and search for the trends that were making waves during the time period from 2015 to 2020. Based on your research, what sectors do you think would have performed well?

The benefits of thematic investing

So why is thematic investing popular? Let's take a look at some of its benefits.

- *Alignment with megatrends*

   Thematic investing enables investors to align their portfolios with the major forces shaping our world. Megatrends such as technological innovation, climate change and demographic shifts can drive long-term growth and provide a resilient foundation for investment strategies.

- *Long-term growth potential*

  By focusing on themes with long-term growth potential, thematic investors seek to capture the compounding effect over time. They position themselves to benefit from trends that are expected to persist or intensify in the coming years.

- *Innovation and disruption*

  Many thematic investments are centred around innovation and disruptive technologies. Investing in these themes can provide opportunities to participate in the growth of companies at the forefront of change.

- *Impactful investing*

  Thematic investing often aligns with investors' personal values and societal objectives. For instance, investing in themes like clean energy and sustainability allows investors to contribute to environmental and social goals while pursuing financial returns.

Challenges in thematic investing

While thematic investing has its merits, it also comes with its share of challenges and considerations and it's important to be aware of these:

- *Volatility and risk*

  Thematic investing can be subject to significant volatility, especially when themes are highly dependent on rapidly changing technologies or market dynamics. Investors must be prepared for fluctuations in their portfolio values. Many of the companies that had heroic performances from 2020 to 2021 had the largest losses in 2022. Peloton fell 76 per cent and then another 77 per cent. Zoom fell 63 per cent and then another 45 per cent. As themes change, so can profits.

- *Lack of historical data*

  Some thematic investments are relatively new, making it challenging to rely on historical performance data. Investors may need to base their decisions on forward-looking projections and potential future developments.

- *Concentration risk*

  Focusing too heavily on a single theme or a narrow set of themes can expose investors to concentration risk. A downturn in the theme's prospects could have a substantial negative impact on their portfolios.

- *Market timing*

  Thematic investing requires a degree of market timing and an understanding of when a theme is in its growth phase. Entering too early or too late can affect returns.

Peter Lynch, whom I've spoken about already, used to tell a story as an example of retail investors having poor timing with thematic investing. It became so popular he ended up writing it in his book, *One Up on Wall Street*.

When Lynch went to cocktail parties and people asked him what he did for a living he would tell them he was a mutual fund manager. When the market was doing poorly, the person would either change the subject or go and talk to someone else.

When the share market started doing better, some months later, people he met at cocktail parties would find out what he did and then ask for advice on this stock or that stock.

When the market was raging and everyone was making money, no matter what the share, and things began to hit peak exuberance, people would find out what Peter did for a living and they would recommend shares to him! And that's when Peter knew the market was overpriced and he should probably take profits before the next bear market or correction happened.

Thematic investing is a lot like that. When everyone is telling you what the hot share is, the timing to buy that share has probably passed and now it is time to look for the next theme on the horizon.

- *Regulatory and policy changes*

  Themes can be influenced by government regulations and policy changes. For example, healthcare themes may be heavily influenced by changes in healthcare legislation.

  I learned my lesson the hard way here in the healthcare legislation realm. I've spoken on my podcast about how I fancied myself as a penny stock picker in the past and I had a very good season of selecting biotech shares trying to make major pharmaceutical drugs. ('Penny stock' is a US term for companies whose shares trade under $2.) I had five or six good share picks that make quick money, sometimes in a few days, but mostly over weeks and months. One company

I had talked myself into buying a little too much of, ended up getting its drug rejected by the US Federal Drug Administration and the share went from $6 to $0.97 in one trading day — a loss of almost 84 per cent in one day — and within a few months it was bankrupt. Penny share investing is *not* for the faint at heart.

Another example goes back to the COVID-19 pandemic. Regulatory factors and the eventual government-mandated lockdowns had a huge effect on global markets. Some shares profited greatly and some companies went bankrupt. So, thinking through regulatory and policy changes cannot be overstated.

At the end of the day, you might be engaging in thematic investing without really thinking about it if you are trying to make active share buying choices based on the news of the day.

But to determine whether you want to be a more active thematic investor you'll need to decide how up to date you want to be. A great thematic investor follows trends closely, forecasts how long a trend will last and takes action on that information. If you are naturally inclined to make lots of moves in your portfolio and stay up to date on mega trends, this might be a natural fit for you. If you want to set up your portfolio to basically run itself while you run your hectic life, then it probably isn't.

If thematic investing is still not scratching your investing itch, well, there's more to come. In the next chapter I'm going to dig into advanced investing options for those who, like me, enjoy building an investment sweat from time to time. I'm going to touch on trading vs investing, and options. If that sounds like fun to you (like it does to me) then grab your energy drink of choice and flip the next few pages.

Start with this …

Now that we have opened up the idea of thematic investing, spend some time to think back on the following:

* How can global megatrends and world events impact share performance?

* Can you remember the potential benefits of thematic investing?

* What are the potential downsides of thematic investing?

* Think of big events going on right now. Pay attention to news articles and the evening news. What are some megatrend events going on in the investing world?

* Write a few down on a piece of paper or on your phone's notepad. Now think of what ETFs, shares or markets might possibly benefit from those large-scale events. Why would they benefit? How much could they possibly benefit?

8

Advanced strategies

This is where the fun begins. Perhaps that's not a fair comment, but I think investing, if done properly, is boring. If you have adopted one of the many strategies listed in this book on how to start investing you've likely set up a plan that is now on autopilot. Congratulations! You're doing it! Look at you, you little investor, you. Now, are you ready for some fun?

This chapter is for those people who:

- have been investing for a while and need to scratch an itch, or

- are looking to create slightly passive income with the investments they own already, or

- are interested in the basics of trading vs investing (yes, there is a difference; yes, we will talk about it).

A word of warning: like all investing, many of these strategies carry risk. Risk of stressing yourself out and risk of not outpacing the index investments despite a lot of hard work on your end, and of course the risk of losing it all. Enter if you dare.

Trading vs investing

As we begin the advanced strategies chapter, I want to touch on trading vs investing. Investing can be as complicated as you want to make it, but should be as boring as you need it to be. I think we have laid out a pretty solid case as to why, for the majority of both my and Glen's portfolios, we are all about set-it-and-forget-it, dollar-cost averaging into passive index funds. If you do that and add automatic investments each month where you take your emotions out of your investing decisions, then your investing will truly be both powerful in regards to wealth accumulation and boring in regards to effort and mental stimulation. When I am at my best and my portfolio is at its best is when I am sticking to my plan, not trying to time the market and everything is on autopilot.

So whenever I get the itch, and I want to try and outperform the market (even though we've proven in this book that to do so is statistically improbable over the long run), and I am stubborn and I know I will be, I have opened a second, brokerage account. Not for investing, but for trading. This account is much smaller than my retirement and brokerage accounts. Overall, my trading account is 1.5 to 2.5 per cent of my investing portfolio. This is enough to make some trades that I desire and helps me keep my hands off my passive index wealth-building portfolio.

In this portfolio, I partake in options, swings and day trades. To be clear, I use cash secured puts in my brokerage account to buy shares I want to own, but I do the other gambling—I mean trading—in this smaller trading account. (Yeah, I know, I've used a lot of terms here that might mean little to you. But don't worry, I'll explain them shortly. Please sit tight.)

So what is the difference between trading and investing? Besides getting your heart rate up, investing is long term and trading is short term. Investing is for five+ years. Swing trading can be anything under five years but in swing trading you are mainly holding a position for weeks or months. And day trading, as you would know, is trades taken in and out in one day — when things go well. If they don't go well, sometimes a day trade becomes a swing trade and if that slips it becomes an unwanted investment. That's what became popular in 2021 in crypto and was known as 'bag holding'. It's when you thought you would make a quick day trade that went against you, and all of a sudden you are holding worthless crypto that is no longer even a coin. I'm looking at you, Shiba Inu holders!

So if you have a desire to be a day trader, like I do, open up a small account and fund it with enough money to make the trades you want to make. Challenge yourself. Make wise, risk-to-reward decisions. For me that means at least a 1:1 RR on scalps and 2:1 on average day trades and never more than 1 to 2 per cent of my trading portfolio per trade. If you do that, you can have a little fun, make some daily, weekly or monthly money with options or futures, and grow your portfolio while you learn a new skill. There are great free tools you can use to paper trade before you start risking your own real money, which I recommend doing.

Now with that being said, let's have some fun, shall we?

Options fundamentals

An option is another way you can invest in the shares market through your brokerage account without having to buy the actual shares themselves. An option is a contract that gives you the ability to control 100 shares of the asset that underlies it, at a certain price (the 'strike price'), at any time before the date set in the contract (thus the short-term nature of these kinds of investments). You pay a premium for the contract. Options belong to a larger group of securities called derivatives because they derive their value from an underlying asset — anything from shares, to bonds, to currencies or commodities (gold, oil, wheat etc.) — and each option typically holds 100 shares of that asset.

Options, like shares, have two sides to every trade. You may not think about it, but every time you buy a share someone else is selling it to you. Although making trades using a computer may feel like it is only a digital transaction, you are still buying from and selling to another physical party.

There are two types of options: 'call options' and 'put options'. Investors buy call options if they believe the underlying asset's value will rise and buy put options if they believe the underlying asset's value will fall.

If you are buying a call option, this is a 'bullish' position (think back to the 'bull market' concept) and you want to see the share price go up. If you are buying a put option, this is a 'bearish' position (think back to the 'bear market' concept) and you want to see the share price go down.

Essentially, your movements are based around trying to predict how the underlying asset will perform: this is what gives options the 'speculative' descriptor. You can see how this could become an all-consuming game if the options bug gets you. It's an attractive way to make money for some investors as you can profit from the movement of share prices without owning the shares, and you can hedge against shares within your regular investing portfolio.

But, likewise, you risk losing more if the asset that underlies the option contract does not perform as expected.

I keep a little notebook with me and whenever I make an options trade on my brokerage account, I just take a quick peek to double check that my position is in fact the options contract that I want to engage in.

You might want to think of the handy little guide box in figure 8.1 whenever you are thinking about buying or selling any sort of options contract.

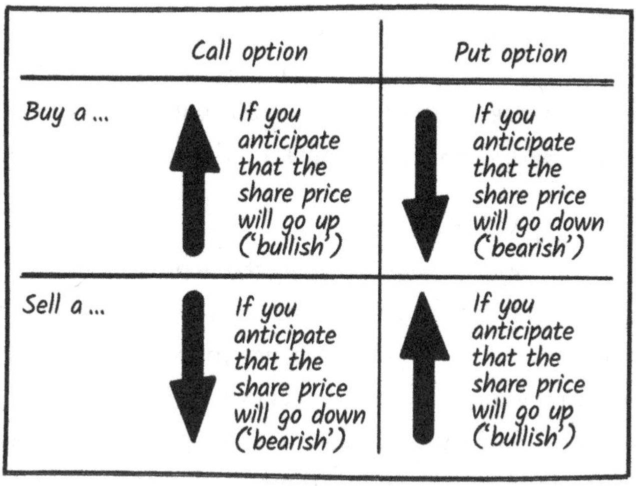

	Call option	Put option
Buy a ...	⬆ If you anticipate that the share price will go up ('bullish')	⬇ If you anticipate that the share price will go down ('bearish')
Sell a ...	⬇ If you anticipate that the share price will go down ('bearish')	⬆ If you anticipate that the share price will go up ('bullish')

Figure 8.1: how to select types of options contracts

This little guide box will help you remember, particularly if you are a beginner, what you want the market to do:

- If you are buying a call option, you want the share or ETF to go up.

- Conversely, if you are selling a call option you want the share or ETF to go down.

- If you are **buying** a put option you want the share or ETF to go down.

- Conversely, if you are **selling** a put option you want the share or ETF to go up.

Examples of options

Let's create an example, and say you are looking at *buying a call option*, with shares as the underlying asset. You pay the premium for the call option contract, and the expiration date outlined in the contract is in three months' time. Naturally, you're watching how those shares are performing each week, along with any other market research you're doing, and deciding if and when you'll take assignment for the lot of 100 shares underlying the call option that you've just paid the premium for. Here's how the example could work out, based on share performance:

- *The share price goes up* over your strike price during the next two and a half months and you can decide to buy the shares at the agreed strike price. Because you're buying the shares at the previously lower price set by the contract, you make an unrealised gain, because the share price has increased but you're basically buying them at a discount. Or you could sell the call option before its expiration date for a profit. Yay for you.

- *The share price goes down* over the next two and a half months. Ultimately, the call option would expire and the options contract would hold no value. Essentially, you've lost out, but only by the amount of the premium you paid in the beginning for the call option. So the maximum loss in this case was the premium you paid. However, if you had purchased 100 shares for $100 each and the shares fell to $0.00 you'd be out by $10 000. But in this case you may have paid $1250 in premium, and you'd only be out the $1250 if the share price fell to $0.00.

Let's now run an opposite example, and say you're looking at *buying a put option*, with shares also as the underlying asset. You pay the premium for the put option contract, and the expiration date outlined in the contract is in three months' time. Again, you're watching how the shares perform, because you want to sell (to close the contract out) at the most opportune time, knowing you've paid a premium for the possibility of making a profit upon sale. Here's how the example could work out, based on share performance:

- *The share price goes down* over the next two and a half months and you can choose to sell the contract before expiration for a profit.

- *The share price goes up* over the next two and a half months. Ultimately, the put option would expire and the shares would hold no value. Essentially, you've lost out, and the out-of-pocket cost would be the premium you paid in the beginning for the put option.

As these examples show, when you buy a call or a put, the maximum loss you can incur is the price that you paid for the option.

Selling an option is another story. You can theoretically have infinite losses when you sell an options contract. So be careful. We will talk about a personal mistake of mine and how to learn from other people's blunders in a bit. First, let's clarify the meaning of a few options-related investing terms.

Speaking Greek?

There are a few terms you need to know when using options and they are almost all Greek words: theta, delta, vega, implied volatility (IV), strike price and expiry date.

Theta refers to the rate of decline in an option over time. All things being equal, options lose money the closer they are to expiration. So theta decay is working against you as a buy and for you as a seller.

Delta measures how much an option can be expected to move for every dollar change in the price of the share or index. I use delta to measure the risk or chance of an option expiring in the money. (ITM, or in the money, is a term used when your option contract is at or over your strike price and therefore you are at risk of being assigned the shares.) A 0.15 delta means there is about a 15 per cent chance of that strike price hitting and an 85 per cent chance it is not happening.

Vega measures an option's sensitivity to implied volatility. In other words, vega measures how much an option's price is expected to change in response to a 1 per cent change in implied volatility.

Not Greek but still important:

Implied volatility (IV) is the market's best guess about how much a share's price is going to jump around in the future, based on what people are willing to pay for options. If traders expect a lot of ups and downs, the prices of options tend to go up. High IV typically means a high options premium.

Strike price is the price you will buy or sell the stock at.

Expiry date is the date the contract expires.

Options strategies in action

Now that you have your handy guide box and we've run some basic scenarios, let's get into a few strategies for options contracts so you can see how your knowledge works in the real world.

Buying a call option

This gives the option holder the right to *buy* 100 shares of a company. It's like saying, 'I have the right to *buy* 100 shares of AAPL stock at $120 per share up until 21 October'. This contract has a market value and can be bought or sold while the market is open.

Let's say you are keen to pick up shares of Microsoft. You believe in the company and think this whole AI thing is going to work out for them. But there's a problem: MSFT is trading over US$350 per share! You want to capture the upside that MSFT has to offer but your portfolio doesn't have the kind of cash to make a substantial shorter term investment in MSFT. Well, you have a few options. (See what I did there? I'm punny.)

What you could do is buy an option with a high delta—think over 0.50. With a delta of 0.50 you are capturing 50 per cent of the movement every dollar Microsoft moves, so for a fraction of the capital needed, you can control 100 shares of MSFT.

So if MSFT is $369 per share, to buy 100 shares of MSFT would cost you $36 900. But if you expect a sizeable move to the upside for MSFT in the next two to three months, you could buy a call option (remembering buying a call is hoping the share goes up) and you can control 100 shares of MSFT for $1805. You will get 50 per cent on the dollar of the movement of the share (all things being equal—which in options they never really are.)

In a perfect trade world, you buy the 0.50 delta option, which is the strike price of $375 per share, and for $1805 in the next three months, if the stock closes above the $375, you should make at least $500.

However, if MSFT doesn't hit $375 in the next 90 days you would take a partial loss, if not an entire loss, on your $1805.

So when you purchased the option you were able to capture some of the upside of MSFT shares by only forking over $1805 and not $36 900.

Selling a call option

Selling a call option should only be done, in my opinion, if you already own 100 shares of the company you are selling the option against. Naked call option selling is crazy and you can lose your shirt, so don't try it.

But if you do own 100 shares of a company, selling a call option — called a covered call (CC) in the scenario — is a way to make some money on top of the possible share appreciation.

I have around six covered call options open right now, as I write this chapter.

One of the CCs I have right now is for a small natural gas company in the United States. I own 300 shares of the company at $42 per share. I've been selling weekly covered calls against those shares and collecting a weekly premium for my part in the contract.

When you sell a covered call you are committing yourself to sell 100 shares of a company at a set price point. My strike price for this week was $48 per share. The price of the stock last week when I sold the call option was $45. So I was betting that the share price would not go over $48 per share by next Friday. And it came really close, but by Friday at 4 pm the price was $47.56 and therefore I was not forced to sell my shares. I kept the $35 in weekly options premium per contract and I am free to sell another contract next week if I so choose. Which I will. ☺

Helpful hint: be careful selling a covered call on a share you are underwater on, unless you are okay selling your stock at a loss. If you bought a share at $40 and it fell to $30, and you sold a CC at $35 and it went back up to $42, well, you lost out on that $2 per share, which on 100 shares is $200. And you actually lost another $500, because you owned the shares at $40.

Buying put options

Investors and traders buy put options for various reasons, and it often depends on their overall market outlook and specific objectives. Here are two quick scenarios and reasons why someone might buy a put option:

1. You think the stock or ETF is going to fall in price. That is the main reason people buy puts. Whenever you see a day trader celebrating on TikTok, they probably bought a put option (and they are also probably exaggerating their wins).

2. Larger institutions with big positions in a share may also hedge their position with a put option. And smart retail investors can do the same. If they hold a significant amount of a particular share and want to protect against a decline in its value, buying put options can limit their downside risk. As your shares fall, the put option gains value and mitigates your downside while you still own the stock for future upside.

Cash secured puts (CSPs)

CSPs have been my go-to 'passive income' generator over three years. I use the quote marks because there is some work to it, but once you've figured out and developed your plan it is, in my mind at least, passive income. We will talk about my plan in a second but let's start by learning what a CSP is.

A CSP is when an options seller looking to make money from an option premium sells a put option on a stock or asset and then the brokerage firm sets aside an amount of money in case the option seller gets 'assigned'. Getting assigned in the CSP world means the option has fallen to your selected strike price and you now need to buy 100 shares of the stock that you sold the CSP on.

Imagine you're making a deal with someone to buy their shares. Here's how it goes.

1. *Making the deal:*

   - You tell someone, 'Hey, if you ever want to sell your shares at a certain price, I'm your buyer'. And they say, 'Yeah? Well, I'll pay you right now to agree to that deal in the future'. And then they give you a smaller set price to agree to the terms.

2. *Putting your money where your mouth is:*

   - To prove you're serious, you set aside some cash. It's like saying, 'I've got the money to buy those shares if you want to sell them to me when they hit our agreed-upon price'.

3. *Now two things can happen:*

   - If the share prices stay higher than the agreed price, nothing much happens. You keep the cash you set aside.

- If the share prices drop and they decide to sell to you at the agreed price, you're ready because you saved up that cash. You use it to buy their shares, and you still keep the bonus cash you got earlier.

Here's a simple example.

Let's say you promise to buy shares of Bradley Enterprises for $50 per share from someone. They pay you $75 for making this promise. You put $5000 ($50 per share x 100 shares) in your piggy bank just in case they want to sell. Now, two things can happen:

1. If the share price stays above $50, you keep the $75 they gave you, and that's it.

2. If the share price drops below $50 and they decide to sell, you're good to go. You use the $5000 in your brokerage account to buy the shares, and you still keep the $75 they paid you.

So, it's like making a deal, proving you're serious by setting aside cash, and either earning a little bonus or getting the shares at a good price if things work out. People like this strategy because it's a careful way to trade shares and might let you grab them at a discount.

My plan is as follows:

I sell weekly CSPs. I only (because I learned my lesson the hard way, as I always do) sell CSPs on companies I want to own. You don't want to sell a CSP just for a good premium; you want to make sure you would like to own the stock, and at a better price than it is today. I stick to the 0.15 to 0.20 delta for selecting my strike price. Each Friday I buy back and sell new CSPs at the same 0.15 or 0.20 delta.

Here's a typical example from my weekly CSPs.

Sell the $30 strike on INTC at the 0.20 delta for a premium of $18.

Sell the $120 strike on AMZN at the 0.15 delta for a premium of $42.

Sell the $17 strike on RIVN at the 0.20 delta for a premium of $11.

So in that week I had to park away $3000 for Intel, $12 000 for Amazon and $1700 for Rivian stock in case I was assigned by the next Friday. I collected $71 in premiums for seven days of risk, making a combined 22 per cent annualised return that week. In other words:

$3000 + $12 000 + $1700 = $16 700

$18 + $42 + $11 = $71

$71 / $16 700 = 0.0042515

0.0042515 × 52 weeks = 22.10 per cent

I am very happy with a 22 per cent annualised return. Since I have a list of shares that I want to own and I know I am comfortable with the 0.15 to 0.20 delta, it is quick for me to open my brokerage account and make these three trades once a week on Friday. If all the numbers stayed the same, the $16 700 in my brokerage will grow an extra (almost) $3700 over a year.

But what happens if I get assigned? Sometimes you want to get assigned — for instance, if you're looking at a share chart and a favourite company of yours is trading at $25 per share. If you know you'd love to own it at $20 per share and are planning on buying, then you could sell a cash-secured put on that share at the $20 strike price. You would then receive the premium, and if it falls to the $20 strike, you'll get paid to buy the share at the price you were planning on buying it at anyway. If it doesn't hit your strike by expiration you can sell another cash-secured put, wait and collect premiums until it does.

Investing in action

Let's put you to the test. Over the next week, go to your brokerage account, find a share you'd like to own, click on the options tab, find the delta on the selling side and find out how much you could get paid to wait to buy the share at the 0.20 delta—let's say three months from now.

The wheel

But what happens if you don't have a certain share price in mind? You don't mind owning the company for the long term, but you also want to create weekly or monthly income in the meantime. In this case, I combine my strategy of cash-secured puts and covered calls — something Wall Street has labelled 'the wheel'.

The wheel is an options strategy that involves both a cash-secured put and a covered call. It starts with selling an assigned cash-secured put. Sometimes you'll want to get assigned and sometimes you won't plan on being assigned — but in this instance you are, so here's an option for you:

- *Step 1:* Sell a cash-secured put near the money, meaning choose a high delta strike price that is close to the current share price.

- *Step 2:* Collect the premium for selling the covered call.

- *Step 3:* Get assigned 100 shares of the stock.

- *Step 4:* Sell a covered call against those 100 shares at a price above your purchase price.

- *Step 5:* Collect the premium for selling the covered call.

- *Step 6:* Keep selling covered calls until you get assigned again and your shares are sold off.

- *Step 7:* Repeat steps 1–6.

The options wheel is illustrated in figure 8.2.

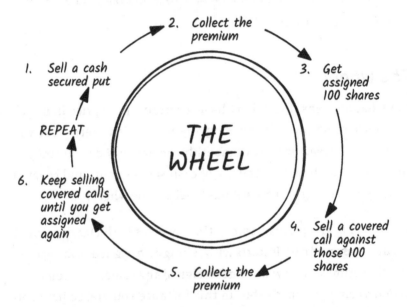

Figure 8.2: the options wheel

An ideal market for the options wheel is a slightly bullish to flat market without a lot of volatility. If the market is too bullish you will most likely get assigned too often; if it is too bearish then you are at risk of getting assigned below your purchase price. So a flatter market without much volatility is recommended. With careful selection in delta prices, you can pull off the wheel in almost all types of market conditions.

How I use options

I have been trading options regularly for about five years. When I say regularly I mean at the bare minimum I've traded some type of options contract at least 10 times a week. So to extrapolate that: 52 weeks, 10 options contracts on average per week, five or so years ... I've bought and sold a *lot* of options contracts. Some worked out well; others not so great. In fact, let's start with a not-so-great story as a word of caution.

That time I almost lost my house, kind of, not really, but almost could have ...

A few years ago, I wrote an options contract called an iron condor (that is, a four-legged options contract where you want the share price to land in between two preselected numbers). Almost like if you were at the roulette table and you made a bet on the second 12th you win, as long as the number doesn't go below the first 12th or above the third 12th.

I wrote the iron condor on the ETF QQQ, which tracks the NASDAQ 100, the largest 100 stocks listed on the NASDAQ stock exchange. This multiple-option contract packaged together as one iron condor paid me $45 per contract and lasted for seven days. To keep the full $45, I needed the QQQ to close just one cent above $325 per share. When I started this contract, the QQQ was trading near $350 per share. Statistically, according to options makers, the chance of QQQ falling to the strike price of $325 in seven days was only 15 per cent.

Well, a few bad news events happened in the share market over the next five days and my option was ITM — in the money — which, as a seller of an options contract, you rarely want to see. I was now faced with the option of buying myself out of this contract for about $300. So my $45 gain was turning into a $300 loss. By Friday afternoon (remember I needed this to close one cent above $325 by Friday at 4 pm) the QQQ had come back up to $323 per share and it looked like it might reach my $325 strike, which meant I would keep the $45 and not have to buy it out. But to be safe I put an order in the computer to buy the option back and lose the $300. I then closed my computer and jumped into the pool.

Saturday morning at 7 am I opened my email and saw that I had been assigned –200 shares of QQQ and I was actively shorting the NASDAQ 100! Shorting is *not* suggested. When you are planning on the market falling, you can 'short' shares of a company you do not own to profit on the fall of the share price. Essentially, when you are shorting, you are borrowing shares from someone else during this short.

When I had closed my computer on Friday around 1 pm, my order was set to a limit order, meaning it would only engage if it hit that limit, and when I hit 'Send' the price fell a little and never got back to that limit. So my order never went through, and three of the four option contracts expired worthless. However, one option buyer wanted to hold me to the contract and therefore I had bought (without knowing or wanting to) $65 000 in QQQ short shares (which is when you make money if the market falls and lose money if the market goes up).

My broker's options trading desk opened at 6 am on Monday morning. It was Saturday at 7 am, and it was my 40th birthday.

To say it was a stressful weekend was an understatement: entertaining people at the surprise party that my wife had put together, while at the same time wondering how much I was going to lose trying to make $45!

After two days of barely sleeping, I got on the phone with the options desk at 6 am on Monday morning. The nice agent explained my situation and was compassionate with me, but told me I needed to wait till 9.30 am to make any movement in my account.

At 9.30 am eastern time in the United States, I logged on to my computer to face the consequences. At market open the QQQ started to fall. I watched with my finger on the 'Buy' button to buy back my active short of –200 shares. By 9.45 am my accidental short ended up making me $2035. Yes, this story luckily had a happy ending, but let me tell you the $2035 was *not worth* the stress of that weekend.

If you are going to engage in options trading you *must* know the full picture of what can happen. I hope my story helps scare you away or makes you interested enough to keep reading.

O O O

There are many other advanced options strategies — from credit spreads, to the collar, to iron condors — but I think these will have to wait for another book. This one's called the *Quick-start guide to investing* after all. Let's make a deal: if this book does well, I will put advanced-advanced options strategies and futures trading into the next book. ☺

It may be challenging to have a broker set you up with an options trading account in Australia due to the complex nature of this world and the regulatory framework. For example, the CommSec Options Trading account will have some restrictions and you will need to apply for various trading levels. You may also need to provide evidence that you are competent and there may be monthly fees for some option trading accounts and features between brokers. It's important to note that there are currently only 99 securities that can be used for options trading on the ASX. Again, Glen's personality does not care for this type of fun. And to that, I say, he is boring.

In chapter 9, Glen and I are going to wrap all of this up. We've covered a lot, and the best step is figuring out what to actually do next. So let's work through that final phase together ...

Start with this ...

Well that was fun! When reflecting back on this chapter, consider the following:

* How does 'trading' differ from 'investing'?

* Could you explain to someone else what an option is and how options work in action?

* What can you learn from my tragic yet saved personal experience?

9

Your investing constitution (Glen)

Company constitutions, or trust deeds, are the founding documents of how an entity should operate. The entity must at all times operate in accordance with what is set out in the document and at times, it needs to be referred back to in order to find a solution to a possible issue or opportunity that may come up. This document is broad and covers a lot of scenarios; however, it is seldom changed. You may also decide you have two different constitutions, one for a goal and one for future wealth building.

This may be a useful tool to complete and have at hand should you be distracted, markets get volatile (in the short term) and you need to get back to what you're doing and the guard rails you have in place. This is why the goal and your 'why' *must* be rock solid because you will need to return to this as your anchor for investing.

Personal investing constitutions

Here are some examples of personal investing constitutions.

Now, can you have a turn at forming your own personal investment constitution? Download the printable PDF template using the QR code on page 204.

Table 9.1: Example 1

Personal investing constitution: Personal wealth	
Date	September 2024
Name (age)	Rebecca (28)
Goal	To live on less than I earn and invest the rest of my money outside superannuation for long-term wealth creation. This will give me the option to cease work before the superannuation preservation age or replace part of my income with my own non-retirement assets.
The 'why'	I grew up in an environment where my parents had money but spent it all. They did not invest for their future and I want to change my family tree. It stops with me.
Time horizon	20 years
Asset allocation	At least 80% growth assets
Ownership structure & vehicle	Own name, Superhero investment platform
Investment strategy	90% three-ETF portfolio 10% made up of individual shares
Other strategy considerations	May stop single share investing if life gets too busy to care or due to lack of interest.
Allocation of portfolio to single shares, advanced strategies, thematic investing or alternative assets (crypto currency etc.)	5–10%, with no more than 2% being cryptocurrency

Personal investing constitution: Personal wealth	
Purchase frequency	Fortnightly into the cash account as per pay cycle; then monthly trades on the first open market day of each month.
Investment selection & target weighting	Australian domestic equity: IOZ 50% International equity: IVV 30% Australian domestic bonds: IAF 10% Individual companies: 10%
Rebalance tolerance +/−	5–10%
Rebalance frequency	Quarterly on the first open market day
Reinvestment of dividends / distributions	Paid to cash account, money reinvested each quarter

Table 9.2: Example 2

Personal investing constitution: Retirement savings	
Date	September 2024
Name (age)	Jake (49) & Sarah (45)
Goal	To maximise our retirement savings to allow us to travel twice per year after age 60 and have a dignified retirement without financial restrictions.
The 'why'	Bringing up a family of three children has been financially challenging. Travel has always been a goal; however, the money was always tight as we prioritised extra-curricular activities and sports for the kids. We are in good health and love our careers; however, we want to look at ceasing full-time work by age 60.
Time horizon	At least 15 years
Asset allocation	70% growth for Jake 90% growth for Sarah

(continued)

Table 9.2: Example 2 *(cont'd)*

Personal investing constitution: Retirement savings	
Ownership structure & vehicle	Current superannuation accounts for each: Jake: Australian Super Sarah: Aware Super
Investment strategy	Jake: Balanced Sarah: High-Growth Socially Conscious
Other strategy considerations	Each year, review balances and contributions and look at superannuation splitting to ensure accounts are equal. In June each year, consider if further tax deductible personal contributions can be added to each account (up to the concessional contribution cap).
Allocation of portfolio to single shares, advanced strategies, thematic investing or alternative assets (crypto currency etc.)	n/a
Purchase frequency	Purchases as per employer contribution deposits.
Investment selection & target weighting	Jake: Balanced; target is 75–80% growth Sarah: High-Growth Socially Conscious; target is 88% growth
Rebalance tolerance +/–	Automatic within the fund
Rebalance frequency	Automatic within the fund
Reinvestment of dividends / distributions	Automatic within the fund

Table 9.3: Example 3

Personal investing constitution: Investment for niece	
Date	September 2024
Name (age)	Mel (27)
Goal	To invest for my niece, Lily (currently aged 4), so one day she has a home deposit as a gift from me.
The 'why'	My partner and I have decided we don't want children, so we love spending time with my only niece, my sister and brother-in-law and have decided that quality time and investments growing in the background are better than buying superficial gifts.
Time horizon	Likely after age 22 for Lily, so 18 years
Asset allocation	90% growth 10% defensive
Ownership structure & vehicle	Investment bond, Generation Life
Investment strategy	100% single multi-sector, multi-asset allocation fund
Other strategy considerations	Will need to hold it for at least 10 years; account in Mel's name, Lily as beneficiary.
Allocation of portfolio to single shares, advanced strategies, thematic investing or alternative assets (crypto currency etc.)	n/a
Purchase frequency	Monthly contributions via direct debit
Investment selection & target weighting	100% Vanguard Diversified High Growth (VDHG)
Rebalance tolerance +/–	Automatic within the fund
Rebalance frequency	Automatic within the fund
Reinvestment of dividends / distributions	Automatic within the fund

Book resources

Follow the QR code for the downloadable PDF of the personal investing constitution template, to watch a video of Glen explaining his sound financial house in greater detail and more. We also provide a service (Australian residents only) to recommend you to a trusted financial adviser or mortgage broker should you be after one of these professionals.

Over to you

We have covered a lot of ground and we do hope you are encouraged to get started with investing, tweak your portfolio if it has drifted or get serious again about building wealth.

Investing can be seen as both an art and a science, requiring a blend of patience, knowledge and strategy. We touched on the essentials of broad-based index funds, basic portfolios, valuing individual companies, setting your investment strategy and understanding the best ownership structure. It's also crucial to understand the trade-off between risk and return, coupled with your time horizon. This means you do not invest in a vacuum, and each part of the investing world will impact another.

○ ○ ○

We hope you are excited to get, or continue to be, invested. Our goal has been to educate you on the macro topics of investing and to inspire you to reignite a passion that may have been dormant for a while or trigger a fresh passion that you never had for investing.

Throughout the chapters, we believe we have made it clear that you need to do things in the right order. The quick-start guide to investing could be seen as follows in figure A:

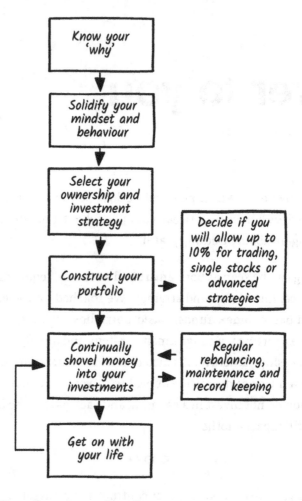

Figure A: The pathway to your investing

Get your house in order

Stop! Before you invest any money at all—or, if you already invest, before you invest anymore—please go back and really look at your financial situation. Get it strong before you commit money to investing. This could be clearing consumer debt (credit cards, personal loans, buy-now-pay-later), funding your emergency fund or even setting up a spending plan so you know exactly how much you have free to invest.

Your 'why'

What is money to you? What do you believe about money? Why are you investing to start with? These questions must have an answer before you commit money to your investing account. If you're unsure and want to build wealth with money you don't need now, that's also okay, but you need to have some conscious thought about your 'why' and your goals, as this is the basis of any strategy that you develop.

Your mindset

Do you have your own personal conviction about your investing, money and even life? Your mindset around investing and money needs to be rock solid so when you hear someone tell you to do something because they do it, you don't change a thing because your situation is set up correctly for you! This also helps if you're part of online forums, listening to podcasts or reading investing books. Your mindset needs to be so firm that you can pick hype vs substance when it comes to investing and other opportunities. Just because everyone is doing it does not mean it's a good thing for you to do.

Setting your strategy

An effective investment strategy is personalised and aligned with your financial goals, risk tolerance and investment horizon. Whether you're saving for retirement, a child's education or building wealth, your strategy should dictate how you allocate your assets across different investment vehicles. It may be considered essential to have a balanced mix of shares (or ETFs), bonds (or fixed interest) and other assets to mitigate risk. Regularly reviewing and adjusting your portfolio to stay aligned with your goals is also a crucial part of your strategy. Your strategy will help you stay the course if things get rough out there and your emotions are tempted to take over! This goes hand-in-hand with having a sound mindset.

Ownership structure

Understanding the best ownership structure for your wealth building and investments can have significant implications for taxes, estate planning and asset protection. Options include individual or joint accounts, superannuation, investment bonds, trusts and companies. Each has its advantages and considerations, particularly concerning tax efficiency and control over the assets. Before you pull the trigger with significant wealth (for example, if you were to receive an inheritance), please seek professional advice around the ownership of your investment vehicle. This will help you determine the most advantageous structure for your situation.

Broad-based index funds

Broad-based index funds are foundational to a well-rounded investment portfolio. These funds track the performance of a specific index, such as the ASX 200, S&P 500 or thematic indexes and provide investors with diversified exposure to a wide array of companies. The beauty of index funds lies in their simplicity and effectiveness. They offer a low-cost way to invest in the stock market, reducing the risk associated with picking individual companies. Over the long term, index funds have historically provided solid returns, making them an excellent choice for both novice and experienced investors.

Valuing and investing in individual companies

For those inclined to take a more hands-on approach with their investing or just to keep the interest alive, valuing single companies is a critical skill. This involves analysing a company's financial health, market position and growth prospects. Key metrics such as the price-to-earnings (P/E) ratio, earnings growth and dividend yield can provide valuable insights. However, it's important to remember that 'stock picking' requires research, a deep understanding of market cycles and a higher tolerance for risk. Your goal may be to identify undervalued companies that have the potential for significant growth. A note to remember is to have your own guardrails in your life and make it part of your investment constitution that you will not have more than, say, 10 per cent of your portfolio allocated to individual companies.

Advanced concepts, trading and speculation

The key with advanced concepts, alternative/speculative asset classes, day trading and options trading is again to have solid guardrails in place. We want you to be engaged and dialled in to your investing; however, you need to understand that the best thing you can do for your future wealth is buy and hold good, broad-based indexes for the long term. We believe past performance of such indexes are a great indication of future performance, if held for long enough! We both love doing advanced strategies and some wild stuff, but we have strong guardrails because these strategies may flush you if you're not careful, and you don't want your whole portfolio allocated to such endeavours!

Your turn

The key to successful investing is to start now, but not to rush into it all at once. Begin with small, manageable steps, focusing on education and building a solid foundation. Reread parts of this book and highlight the crap out of it (unless you borrowed it from the library!). As you gain experience and confidence, always be mindful of your long-term goals and risk tolerance in concert with your strategy and personal investing constitution.

Remember, the journey to financial independence is a marathon, not a sprint. Patience, persistence, a well-thought-out strategy and time are your best allies. Investing is a powerful tool for building wealth, but it requires a thoughtful approach and a commitment to ongoing engagement (even if quarterly!). By understanding the basics of aspects such as broad-based index funds, diversification, sectors and the importance of a personalised strategy with an appropriate ownership structure, you can navigate the investment landscape with confidence. Take it step by step, seek professional advice when needed and remember:

- The best time to start investing is now.

- One dollar invested today could be five dollars for future you.

- Investing is not gambling. At no point have we suggested that there is any game of chance involved with buying quality profitable companies even through broad-based indexes.

- If you don't respect money, you won't be able to control it no matter how much you have.

We wish you much success with your financial future.

Yours in investing,

Glen & Nick

Join us on Instagram
@thisismoney.podcast (Glen) and
@personalfinancenomad (Nick)

We live on opposite sides of the world, but at least once a year we get to say hi. This was us in New Orleans for FinCon 2023! (Glen left, Nick right).

Keep up-to-date with the **this is money** and **this is investing** podcasts

Disclosures

In the spirit of transparency, we have detailed the following associations or perceived conflicts with real-world companies or brands we have used as examples in the book (listed alphabetically). The following disclosures are accurate at the time of print.

Glen

Holds the following investments mentioned in this book:

Bitcoin, IOZ, IVV, VAP, VDHG

Has active accounts with:

Generation Life, Superhero

Glen's business, which hosts the podcasts *this is money* and *this is investing* and associated social-media platforms, has had the following companies pay to advertise or has been paid by them for corporate speaking:

Amazon, AwareSuper, Commonwealth Bank, GlobalX, Microsoft, Moomoo, Sharesies, Sharesight, Superhero, Vanguard.

Nick

Holds the following investments mentioned in this book:

AMZN, Bitcoin, BRK/B, COST, GOOG, MSFT, QQQ, SPY, TSLA.

Index